Faith Walk

By: V. Kollie

Faith Walk is a journey lived and currently living by the graciousness of God. The breakdown of faith is of many different versions told by those, including myself, who have testified about their faith journey. The way God has been not only in my life but in the lives of others I have encountered have been quite miraculous and wondrous. Some testimonies will be told while others will be kept for it's not my place to disclose. Faith Walk is not about criticizing the lives people are living currently nor have overcome in the past. For this is my life journey I choose to share with those who are willing to listen and not judge for their own personal gain. Faith Walk is a real life experience along with past virtues that have been proven in today's world which many have failed to see and understand. For this is my walk of faith not what others want me to have. For we are our own people and decide what life we live. No man can control nor have a say in that matter! For those who believe there is a God, let him have the final say to the end of your day without remorse, conflict, confusion or regret. Just know he will not leave you astray for his plan is far greater than any purpose you yourself can set forth in life. Not many people can talk about their faith as they walk within it. Some will walk without a word while others walk and talk at the same time like professional trainers. I choose to walk and not speak because those who I speak to will either not understand or misguide me in some way. Those who walk and talk can be understood but also misguided by those they trust and feel will never steer them wrong. Then that's when they're wrong and go through a whole self sabotage and coming to God to redirect them back to where they were like come on. That's the "worry faith", not the "I trusted God in the beginning" faith. We all know better and can do better let alone treat and appreciate God's love, kindness, guidance, generosity and blessings better! Yet we choose otherwise! We choose to abuse to take him for granted yet try to say how worthy we are for his forgiveness. Insane we are, crazy we must be and humans we shall remain. For he knows all these things about us and still treats us the same no matter how different we treat him. Faith Walk is about realizing mistakes made in life and becoming more self aware of who we are, of who I am as a woman and as a child of God. As we journey, please keep an open mind, open heart and open spirit. God bless and let's walk.

God doesn't give us more than our flesh can bare. He gives what he knows our spirit can conquer. That's why it is written " he will not give more than ye can bare" for it is meant for our spirit to show faith and overcome. While in flesh, many will face obstacles they see are hard to overcome. They seek a helping hand from others that are told of the obstacles but do not know how to overcome. That's when opinions of others' advice come into play. Those who think they can help are not helping, those who have overcome this type of temptation have yet to defeat it but still in progress. You know God wants us to come to him first while knowing we seek him last. Which is natural, it's natural normal human behavior. For those who do seek God first and wait on his guidance and wisdom congrats. As for others it is ok, no shame no judgment; for we are still learning as we grow. And we should. You will never stop learning until the day the Lord calls you home. Remember that. On the other hand, most people expect God to provide as soon as they call upon his name. Like he's an ATM machine you place your prayer and blessings start to flow like that's what most people expect. We should all know by now God is a merciful, forgiving loving graceful and trusting God. He provides according to his will, purpose and of course his beautiful timing. Do you trust God enough to know your prayers are heard and answered? Do you believe he loves you so much he allowed his son's life to be given so our sins are forgiven? By his stripes we are healed and free from sins we create and have created? God may not come when you want him but know he will be there right on time! This I believe, for in Proverbs 3:5 says, "Trust in the Lord with all thine heart and lean not unto thine own understanding". I believe he is with me every day, every night, every week, every minute to every second; I believe he is with me even when

I am sad, happy, mad or indifferent. I know God's presence is real! May not feel real to you and maybe you need to spend more time with him but I know he is real to me. Proverbs 3:13 "Happy is the man that findeth wisdom and the man that getteth understanding". Are you happy? Do you honestly feel you are happy? I don't mean what another person does or makes you, I'm talking about, are you happy with God and what he has done for you in this life? Can you open your heart and hands say, "Lord I am happy with you and because of you I am happy with the life ye has given. It may not have been easy but I am grateful it is my life."? Would you be happy if God gave you everything you asked of him? I wouldn't. For I wouldn't have learned from my mistakes, I wouldn't know the meaning of true discipline of my actions nor understand the consequences of my wrongs. So no I wouldn't. Would you? There will be no divine plan for my future, there will be no mercy, grace or even true love and no connection with God whatsoever. I will literally be walking by sight and not by faith! I would rather walk by faith, I would rather have a deeper connection with God more so than any materialistic things or person. I'm coo on that note! There's nothing like having God's love, his wisdom, his guidance, his devotion in my life and even your life! It's amazing to have and to be honest it's an honor! Amen God! I thank you for all you have given me thus far and to come. I thank ye for all the revelation ye have bestowed upon us, allowing us to be part of your grace, mercy and love! For your discipline is far more greater than loyalty shown by those who mean us harm for we cannot see what our spirits see but to only feel what is done. Lord I thank you, for your devotion has taught me amongst others many life's obstacles and temptation but also has rewarded blessings upon those in your will; who hold true to your purpose and rely only on your understanding. For they truly walk by faith in you and not by their own sight! Amen! The joy of his presence, the feeling of his love is more than "ahh" it is as simple as saying "yes Lord here I am". And to meditate on God's word is more than enough to move forward through any hardship, obstacles and/or temptation. Just keep going, don't look back only forward. Do not stumble upon thy own feet my child keep walking, keep believing, and your keep faith! Be strong, be of good courage for I am with you. God has said this to Moses and to Joshua but know it is meant for us too! Watch how he moves mountains, quiet the loudest storms and whispers through the calming winds. Yes, he is truly worth the wait!

You never know how much you miss a person until they are no longer around. Whether it's in passing or simply moving on with your life without them being involved anymore. When a person passes, there's a process we all go through in order to move forward with them no longer being in this world. It's called grieving and most people possibly grieve differently from others. There are many stages of grief depending on the person but some do it more well than others. Like they can handle loss better than some, even though you grieve the best way you know how. There's no rocket science to grief: you feel, you process and you move on day by day, step by step. But let me ask you: What do you seek when you grieve? Do you seek Christ? Do you seek sympathy from those who state they care but never showed it? Do you seek support from others outside of your circle just feel wanted or even thought of? Do you reach out instead of being reached for? Why do it? Why not be content with who has become or becoming? Why must you put forth the energy when it is not necessary let alone wanted? You're just giving it away? But you cry when you're alone and those you reached out are too busy to give you comfort they once said before. You know, 2 Corinthians 1:3-4 states "Blessed be God, even the Father of our Lord Jesus Christ, the Father of mercies, and the God of all comfort; Who comfort us in all our tribulation, that we may be able to comfort them which are in any trouble, by the comfort wherewith we ourselves are comforted of God." Is God not enough comfort? As humans, we do seek more than what is already given. Why not be content with God and his comfort? Those who proclaim their love for God come only from the mouth; those who proclaim more trust in God only come from the mind. Honestly speaking, true love and trust comes from the heart! For your spirit will show a greatness of gratitude and praise for the Lord our God! I know for I have gone through my trials of claiming with my mouth and repeated my mind about how I love and trust God. Yet I was still seeking love, seeking trust from those who barely gave me the time of day let alone said "hi, how you doing?" It was sad and most painful, yes but I come to realize only one who has been there since the beginning and not once changed his patterns, let alone view of me. As light shines within this room, God has been around daily walking with Jesus daily not missing a single beat or a single step! Amen! I am blessed, I am grateful, I am more than aware God stands within me without me having to seek. Now this may or may not offend some people but for those who have literally talked about faith after walking in faith knows what I mean. Psalms 33:12 "Blessed is the nation whose God is the LORD; and the people whom he hath chosen for his own inheritance." They have seen and they have lived. They first and foremost chose God and told their testimonies while praying it will inspire others to do the same. But not all people will listen, not all people will believe or understand. And those who do listen will have opinions of criticism: those who believe and say they understand will be the ones that talk about you behind your back. Calling you crazy and how your life is a mess and/or you need to do better. It's always something barely nothing! It's never just enough! People gotta have something in order to not have nothing but have more than enough! All he wants is us! All God wants is us! But that is asking a lot isn't it? You can give yourself to another person for one night of pleasure but can't give yourself to God for a moment of prayer? If not for a moment how about your remaining time here on earth. Is he not worthy of you? But that guy or girl for 10 seconds of "love"? Just asking. Not judging at all! I just want to know who you find to be more worthy of your time. Psalms 33:18-20 "Behold, the eye of the LORD is upon them that fear him, upon them that hope in his mercy; To deliver their soul from death, and to keep them alive in famine. Our soul waiteth for the LORD: he is our help and our shield." Is seeking the heart of others more worthy or is seeking the heart of God himself more than enough? David was a young man after God's own heart. Yet he went through temptation like us while still seeking God's heart. David's temptation led to the death of his firstborn son, his heir whom he loved the most. David had learned God's heart through the life he lived as king. But he finally understood on the day he died that God's heart was true and pure of love not just for him but for all mankind. No human heart will come close to this! For temptation is far more greater and desirable to the eye that seeks. I seek God's heart, I seek his truth, his wisdom and his love daily. Yet temptation has steered me through the darkness of trials within me. Which I have overcome with faith in my heart yet my mind is troubled. And yet temptation still follows like a winded fart lol. I believe temptation will never leave us, for it keeps us grounded, humbled and teaches us God's grace and mercy. We must learn from our grievances, from our mistakes and from God's word to be humble and show gratitude for life itself. You cannot seek what ye have not yet learned. You cannot embark on a journey set by God with those who are no longer in your path. It's ok to let go. It's ok to have seasonal acquaintances or friends whatever label you have for those individuals. Same goes with family. Just because you are blood related doesn't make them loyal like you, doesn't make them respect you the way you respect them, and it doesn't make them love you the same way you love them. We are all different but bleed the same as our Lord and Savior. You know what I have also noticed? Throughout my life here no one treats you the way you treat them. It's like people have their own twisted version of Matthew 7:12 "Therefore all things whatsoever ye would that men should do to you, do ye even so to them: for this is the law and the prophets". The same goes for Luke 6:31 yet a little different wording "And as ye would that men should do to you, do ye also to them likewise". Both scriptures have the same meaning depending on the person receiving the word and how they interpret. Then again most will realize a person's generosity to be genuine yet lack the understanding of how it makes the other person feel taken for granted. I have often felt that I was too kind, too loving and too giving and will receive the same in return. Well I felt wrong and was in a dark place about it for a while. In those times I received many lies, deceit and advice on what to do next and given run-arounds of when I will be given back to. It was all a headache! And when you're in a relationship, is it expected to ask for something when your mate knows you don't have it? Or should just be given automatically after having many conversations previously? Some will agree, most will disagree and many will be indifferent. Though I can be wrong and most will say I'm being judgmental and really most respectfully I am not. Just speaking on what has been done in my life which may seem similar yet very different in the eyes of many. In those scriptures both Matthew 7:12 and Luke 6:31, as many provide them to be "Do unto others as you want done unto you"; speaks on a certain level to me. And that level is worth. Know your worth and who God has called you to be before you go out and start being a Good Samaritan, then look to reap the benefits of the good you have done. Know what your true intentions are: is it for your own benefit or is it for God's glory? You know I pray, "Please Lord, open the eyes of not only me but of my fellow brother and sisters through Christ for we are somehow closed by the shadow of selfishness and accolades from this world. Open our eyes to see your love, to do your will and to fulfill your purpose from the blessings of which you hath given us day to day moment by moment. We thank ye O' Imanuel for the mercy you have upon us and showed gratitude amongst gratefulness. For our eyes deceive what we hear as our ears believe what we see. This unfortunate gateway to our minds and hearts is misleading and therefore we are somehow losing sight of the victory you have claimed within us, Lord. For this alone should give us strength to move forward stronger in faith and to be more humbled in thy word knowing surely we shall not go without! Father God, you are our provider and I believe in your wisdom and guidance of my life for I cannot speak for the lives of others; it is their faith they must walk and I have learned speaking for those unspoken do come with unexpected consequences. This could be of good courage or of bad misfortune however it depends on who responds and how actions are perceived." You know most people are only meant to be in your life for a season or to be permanent root of your growing tree. The thing is there is no time in these matters and people often get mad when life hits with a certain amount of curveballs. But how can we not? To some it is not fair and others know we have some control but not overall for no man has control over life obstacles. It's how you run thy course when ye shall conquer. We must live the life God intends for us to live. It may not be perfect in our eyes but it is perfect enough because he can see our good enjoyments of life and he can also see the bad moments we encounter in life. Yet he has given us this will to be free and to know what is good and bad and indifferent but also to trust in his word know he is God! Know he will be there whether you can or cannot see nor feel his presence. Have faith in him!

    Have you ever noticed how irritating you can be until you not only irritate another person but also yourself at the same time? I can admit, I am irritating and also annoying but mostly irritating. This is something I know I am currently working on but also struggle amongst other things I struggled to overcome. For instance, I have struggled to overcome depression. I am struggling with some forms of anxiety to which I do not know why. And lastly I am struggling to overcome my picking disorder which has been a constant battle since a young age. For this I do not understand nor can explain but will try to the best of my ability. It's a constant battle for me and I pray daily although denouncing the spirits that are holding me to these things I wish to be free. In the past I have spoken briefly about having "thorns" or a "thorn". I have learned this from a sermon I have attended and the pastor was preaching about Paul and how he was given a thorn from God by a messenger from the enemy. I feel as though my struggles: you know the anxiety and picking are to keep me humble so I do not lose sight of who God is calling me to be. 2 Corinthians 12:7-9 " And lest I should be exalted above measure through the abundance of the revelations, there was given to me a thorn in the flesh, the messenger of Satan to buffet me, lest I should be exalted above measure. For this thing I besought the Lord thrice, that it might depart from me. And he said unto me, My grace is sufficient for thee: for my strength is made perfect in weakness. Most gladly therefore will I rather glory in my infirmities, that the power of Christ may rest upon me." Amen. I have prayed more than three times for these to be away from me and yet I have learned to cope and ground myself so I do not lose control nor let myself be taken over by this. I admit at times I do lose myself and have relapsed many times. For which I become ashamed and feel as though I should not be looked at because of what I picked at. Though my wife has been very supportive in this matter, I have my moments which I pray throughout the day. I thank God everyday for my "struggles" as I called them before and give him praise for I am not as bad as I was many years ago and I now have someone who loves me for me and not my looks or smart whits lol. I am truly blessed beyond mantras and affirmations most people rely on day to day. Again, not passing judgment, do what is of comfort to you because to me God is my comfort and for that I am grateful to be uncomfortable. Even speaking on this is very uncomfortable for me, very private yet I must speak on what holds me in order to free another somewhat like me. I say this because the presence of God is comforting but that doesn't mean for us to be comfortable for we do not know God's divine plan nor have say in his will nor can we fully carry out his purpose unless he tells us to. For those who are comfortable, God bless you and may he continue to show his mercy and grace upon you. For I know being comfortable is like going on a rollercoaster ride with padded leather seats and being served drinks and appetizers at the start. And this may look good and feel great but is sickening when the ride is over. Then you go again and again and again until you're dark in the face, unrecognizable and ready to get off mid ride because you're tired; too ill to carry yourself further on to see the end again. When does it stop? or Do you want it to stop? The choice is yours. May heaven smile upon you always. God Bless.

    You know the sadness of reality, is when you realize that you'll never be enough. Especially when you're trying to be enough for those who do not recognize let alone appreciate you. You see, my spouse has these two sisters whom my spouse thought she had within her corner. But my spouse soon realized all she had was God in her corner, especially when God had called her to remove herself not only from them but other walks in her life. The sad thing is even when my spouse explained herself of why her sisters ignored her cry and only thought of them. They didn't even acknowledge the pain, the hurt my spouse was trying to express let alone share with her siblings. I too have encountered this very same experience but in a different aspect. My sister and I have a "distanced relationship". The same goes for me and my brother; we barely converse or keep in touch on a "regular" basis. It is more of a "see you when I see you" basis for my brother and I. As for my sister, I have always admired and loved my sister however I can't say if the feeling is mutual. For that is something for her to explain herself. For me, I have always felt like I am invisible but not invisible when it comes to my sister. Henceforth my sister and I do not have a bond like most siblings have with each other. Same goes for my brother. I have learned to accept what I do not have nor can create especially if you are not on the same wavelength as them. Once I realized these things, that's when you start to feel yourself separating naturally. One day, I told my sister that I was stepping away meaning removing myself from her, my nephews and nieces; which is all not a big deal, seeming how I barely see, let alone spoke to any of them expect when the trio wanted to come over or if the "blue moon" struck my nephew wanted to come over. Well, my sister didn't like that. She was not too thrilled, she showed up to my house and called our mom. Now we all get this gut feeling, sort of like an intuition of something is going to happen. I tried to brush it off but this was a strong feeling. Before you know it, my oldest is like, "Ma! Auntie here!" Instant eye rolling while trying to fix the hallway light and smoke detector here goes my sister at the top of the stairs. So she goes, "We gotta talk!" I'm like "Hello to you too and hold on, I'm trying to get this light together and putting this smoke detector back on the ceiling." So I finished and went into my bedroom, the door was open and she sits on my blue workout ball which I call "Bluey". I sit on the bed across from her and Bluey. Then she says, "I am not sure what is going on. Please explain because I had to call momma and was like " I don't know ma! I don't know what's wrong or what I did but I refuse to have my baby sister mad at me." So I came over so we can talk. So like what did I do?" Instantly my mind was like "Oui!" but very calm, no emotions really. I began to explain, at least I thought I was being understood; I said "Truth be told big sister, we haven't been very close and I understand you are going through alot but I am just distancing myself from those who don't show me the same of what I give them." Her face was giving the look of "ok" but very confused. Mind you the room was a bit dark but the hallway light was on and she was sitting in a darkened spot of the room but the light was radiating more on the side of the bed where I sat. So it was a bit challenging to make out her facial expressions. She responded to what I had said but it was more of her expressing herself as if I had done her wrong. She did admit she hasn't been her best sister and went into details about her parenting her kids and then she explained how I made her out to be a bad Auntie. To which I replied no! Granted yes my oldest did ask her to take her to get her ears pierced and yes a couple weeks has gone by since her asking and she started to ask me to take her. It just so happened when my oldest was asking me about it again for the tenth time; Mind you all again it has been a few weeks already; my friend was there and she overheard and we briefly discussed it. My friend then asked my oldest do she want her to take her to get her ears pierced and that's when my oldest said yes and then my youngest wanted to go too. So I explained that to her to which she did not like my response but that's what happened. Then we discussed other matters and she commended me on not letting my kids have their own phone because what her middle child has displayed recently and I was like thank you. Then there was silence for a brief moment. Then I said to her, " We have never been close for real. And honestly I feel as though we know each other but really don't know each other. I love you and always will." To which she responded " Well, I don't know what you want me to say or do. I can't give you my best right now. I just can't right now." Now guys, my facial expressions say it all and I am surprised she didn't respond to it. My response, "I am not asking for the, "best of you", all I am saying is that we never had a bond and neither do our children. We have all grown apart. It is not fair for me or the trio to keep reaching for something that is no longer there and has a different path." At that point, I was not sure if she understood nor accepted what I had said. She left that night and we haven't spoken for quite some time until recently. She had asked for the trio to come over and stay for a weekend. I declined the offer because truth be told and I have informed her of this: the trio has not been asking for her and when they do it's only because they don't want to be home or go to daycare. It's never a genuine request. Then she brought our grandmother and how she wouldn't want our families to be separated. To me that's a low blow which was easily blocked because she had a point that our grandmother(Lord rest her soul) wouldn't want our family to be divided. However, granny knew how her family was before she passed and yes it was her desire for us to have a tight bond but she knew there was no bond! I explained that to her and also informed her that we all have different lives; and yes we are divided because of the differences in our lives. I believe families should be there for each other through the good, bad and indifferent without being judgmental. There's no love in judgment but there is grace in mercy. For our Lord Jesus knows all about this! Once you realize these things about other people that's when other things around you seem to be a threat. Like there are others more important than you. But when you notice the shift in behaviors towards one another. Then that's when the matters of trust and loyalty come into play. You then decide whether you should stay or you should go; will it be a fling or you go back to where you once came so what was better is now worse than before. Don't get this wrong, I love my sister and I love my family. But if God says for me to move and remove then trust and know thy will be done! However, my sister and I are on much better terms yet still there are some bumps in the road. How the Lord sees fit is how I shall proceed. I love my siblings and pray for the best for both of them.

A lot comes to mind when involving kids. You know raising kids whether by yourself or with whomever you choose to spend your life with can be challenging to accept the way you yourself were raised. It should not be the responsibility of one sibling to raise or watch over their siblings.

Especially if you are all grown and have lives and families of your own. Any parent who raises their child to take care of their other children needs to have several seats and many prayers. I am just speaking. This is not right nor is it fair to that child. I mean is it fair to see one sibling as a party sister and/or the other as a sister dad while the two are just building each other up, supporting one another's habits while the other takes care of what they both lack? Why seek one sibling to be your cook/entertainer/money maker while neither of you does anything except sit there and judge while sitting on a fake pedestal. How fair is it for one sibling to listen to your problems, build you up emotionally and mentally while they are suffering themselves but all you can think of is how your feelings are hurt? Hurt from what?! No harm came upon you so why are you being selfish?! Why should she not be happy just so you can be comfortable? Getting a bit touchy here, lets fall back an inch! Are they aware of what is going on or is it your job to bring forth the documents of explanation? How much more needs to be explained when all is plain and clear. May not seem simple but it is fully explained. Again, all siblings should build each other up, not try to profit or benefit from each other's success! Just be happy for one another and accept each other as you are and for who you are! I know. The irony. The shame. Oh, Lord the horror of such kindness and love to show! However, let me go to my next words of unspoken demise. For my life is spoken, my spouse's life is spoken, my trio lives are spoken! We live by faith not by sight, we trust what the Lord has laid before us the paths unseen which we walk! Let us talk more of faith as we walk to see the glory of God. Amen!

Listen, I am no marriage counselor nor expert on meaningful relationships. What I have learned so far in this life is: if you are going to be with someone please be sure they are who God wanted you to be with and you are with that person for all the right reasons. Be sure you love them with your heart not with your mind, be sure you're attracted to them spiritually and not just mentally, and also show them you care for them the same way you care for yourself; love yourself first before you can love another. Please know God has placed this person in your life for a reason which can be a season but this can be a permanent season or temporary. Know the difference and pay attention to the signs which the Lord will provide. You see the Devil can mimic what your heart desires but he can shadow it as if this person is a gift from the Lord. But you must know, what a person foreshadows in the dark will come to light especially when the other person is a child of God. You see the Devil can only tempt for so long to see if he can get you to turn your faith away from God but once he is unsuccessful then that is when truth is revealed. Do not blame yourself nor question God of "why"; just remember Romans 8:28-29 "And we know that all things work together for good to them that love God, to them who are called according to his purpose. For whom he did foreknow, he also did predestinate to be conformed to the image of his Son, that he might be the firstborn among many brethren." And another on that most people would not read after or just skip to another verse of the bible; Romans 8:30-31 "Moreover whom he did predestinate, them he also called: and whom he called, them he also justified: and whom he justified, the he also glorified. What shall we then say to these things? If God be for us, then who can be against us?". Meaning you may feel as if God has blessed you with this person but come to find out it was the "tricks" of the Devil who wanted you to turn away from God and follow him down a path he tried to create but God….but God has already predestined your path so once you so the light you shall follow. Even with all your hurt and disappointments and feeling as if you are not good enough because you thought…. you thought that this person was for you but really they were against you! And he wanted you to feel low and wanted you to be in a dark place where he foreshadowed but God…..But my God had other plans for he was with you the entire time he was on the path he has set for you and when he shine his light brighter upon your path and saw his light he knew where your faith lied all along. While you thought you were "tricked" you were really being "taught" the goodness of the Lord! Amen! You were being taught the favor of God is more precious than the last date night with whatever their name is or even the last gift you thought was meaningful but really was a Devil's "keepsake" for you to "aww" over. It was for you to forget about any mean words said, for you to forget them hurting you physically and guilting you mentally so they ... .and by they I mean this person and Satan; so they can have brought you down more than what you were feeling and crush what little faith they now think you have. But God....lol, but God o'ye of little faith....but God had his hand over you. But God has his hand on your heart while talking to your spirit and he has his lips to your mind and ears reassuring you victory is mine! Whoa, thank you Lord! Father God I thank you for your wisdom, your lessons teaching me more about life than what I thought I knew but I am still learning. I thank you for your guidance through the Devil's "temptation tricks" for he may have stumbled me but you my Lord have straightened my walk. For you my God have seen my little faith, gave me strength to continue on and not give up from those who have let me down, put me down, dragged my name through mud of the dirtiest land. You my God have strengthened my faith when I thought I was alone and not enough! Yet you showed me Lord that I am enough for you and truthfully I am enough for me; I need no other person to defy who I am when my Lord God and his son Jesus Christ has shown me more love than I can fathom. Romans 8:35-36 "Who shall separate us from the love of Christ? shall tribulation, or distress, or persecution, or famine, or nakedness, or peril, or sword? As it is written, For thy sake we are killed all the day long; we are accounted as sheep for slaughter. Nay, in all these things, we are more than conquerors through him that loved us." Thank you, thus I pray Amen!

    You know, my spouse and I clearly have many differences and we both have love for God but in our own ways. Now, I can't say whether her love for God is the same as mine but we both have a past of struggles when it comes to trust. I trust the Lord with all my soul, my life, my children and my entire being. MY spouse is the same but her trust has wavered for so many years. To which she can explain in her own words but for me I have noticed her waverings in our relationship amongst other things. We have taught each other so much especially when our past seems to reflect in our present. My wife had to learn to not get so mad over what was small to me but huge to her. Not saying we have the most perfect God fearing relationship but we do have our trials and tribulations all with God's wisdom, guidance and consultations. Several consultations. There was a period of time at the beginning of our relationship, where I questioned God with the same questions on steady repeat especially when we had our disagreement moments. The question(s) was, "Why is she here Lord? Why did you put her in my path knowing that to me, I am not the one for her?" Now me and my wife as you all have read before worked together for many years but didn't become good friends until a couple out of those six years later. We worked for the same company; both were supervisors once upon a time then we both moved on to different jobs meaning she left her supervisor's position and I of course got demoted which no hard feelings can't please everybody. However I was able to start school which I have wanted to do but was naturally led to do it by God to complete the tasks he has set for me within this field. My wife went on to help elderly people in their homes and nursing facilities which is what she loves to do. She is a phenomenal caretaker and all of her clients love and appreciate her work ethic. Mind you we are only friends at this point with some interest and scattered dates here and there but it was nothing steady or serious at this time. A new year was approaching and we both were in parts of our lives that were in question of "where do we belong" and "what do you have planned my Lord". The funny thing is God knows so much but will keep you in the dark until his will has come forth and revealed itself unexpectedly. Love you Lord but a heads up would be nice lol. The new year 2019 has started and turmoil was in the air. I was feeling like a used puppy on its way back to the pet store and my wife aka friend at the time was having trouble in what she thought was her home. Of course I didn't know because I worked nights and was focused on school. She called me one night while I was working stating she wanted to see me but her voice was troubled yet sad. I took a break from my job, mind you I was working in a group home and not too far from where she was at. So I go pick her up and take her to my place so she can have some peace and quiet and gather herself and I of course went back to work to finish my shift. Once I got off work, I picked up my trio from daycare and no they weren't shocked or confused to see her because they have all met before on several fun occasions. So the trio were happy to see her gave her hugs and ask her lots of questions lol. It was a pleasant night. I don't know why I am being led to tell our story but here it goes. After the trio had gone to bed, me and her stayed up and we talked. She explained to me what happened in her home between her and her sister and all what was said which was not pleasant but very disturbing at the same time. She also explained how she had a dream before all this took place and of course I explained to her about dreams and how they can be signs from God and to pay attention. She claimed she knows that but she was giving the "benefit of doubt" vibes as if those who are close to her cannot bring most harm. Me, I let it go and prayed to God on what to do next. My friend felt like she was at her lowest but I supported and gave her advice and even helped her increase her hours at her job. She appreciated my help and was very grateful; her and her sister were back on speaking terms but still had some rough patches unsorted. As time goes by, I am close to getting ready for my externship! Nervous but excited. Now the externship did not go as I had thought, especially when you get to an office of a company who is well known for helping students exceed their learning and job skills. Don't get me wrong I learned alot from this office with Promedica but the staff, well some of the staff were good to me while others were rude. However, staying in prayer and keeping my head up my externship only lasted a week and what was told about me was not at all truthful. I felt as if I wasn't good enough because of what was said and I was a disgrace to my teachers who worked hard to educate me to be prepared for this training. When I say my tears were so deeply internal they became external and I don't like to cry in front of people, not even my kids! So that was put on hold and I couldn't start my externship until later which pushed my graduation date back a couple months. I didn't give up though, I just worked more hours at my job until those hours became available. My wife aka friend but now girlfriend at the time was very supportive, even though she was overcoming her obstacles she was there when I didn't ask her to be but she wanted to be there for me. Things were looking good so far and still I was in question of "why she was in my life" and still no answer from God just day by moment ventures. I didn't expect to fall for a woman because I grew up thinking only man and woman should be together. That same sex relationships were highly frowned upon and found to be "disgusting". As Randomlize stated " you don't have to be what the world wants you to be, only be what God has called you to be! For he does not discriminate nor does turn his face from the loves he has created and the love Jesus has died to save!" Hmm. How sweet that he would save a wretch like me. The most love from a person is unexpected from God and why he would create and Jesus died to forgive is the most appreciated unexpected desirable love any human can ask for! If ye dare to ask for more surely do not appreciate nor love our God and his son Jesus Christ. Our relationship was unexpected and it sort of just fell into place like a puzzle with a thousand pieces still being put together. You know I lost faith in the love of another. Don't get me wrong I love God and I love my trio with all my heart but for someone who is not my child whom I gave birth to, it was hard for me to love another person. I didn't expect to be with a woman as stated before due to my upcoming in life and after the disappointments, misguidance and bad advice I just left it alone and became content with living life with just God, my trio and I. Lord knew what he was doing when he heard me but did not answer in the way I expected him to; my faith in his response was stronger than I anticipated. Yet my wife and I were too blind to see his goodness and the love he had for us. For us to be together, we both had many encounters with those who questioned our relationship. We had people who were family and not family make it seem as if we were not "right", that our way of living is not of God and we should rethink our "lifestyle". And yet they do not know what we have been through previously outside of what we tell them; whether it's half or whole situations. Still they stated their opinions as if we were an abomination to God and we are not. To those who said these things or are saying these things may you first consult with God before passing your own judgment upon those he created and knew who they were before they even said "waah" out of their mother's womb! Did God create man and woman? Yes. But did he give the standard that men and women should be together? No, not really. It was man that called woman his wife, not God. God gave man help for he saw the land was too much for man to handle alone and just respected what man has said for man was grateful. I am just speaking. And you see me and my wife both have our own hiccups that we don't want nor need anyone placing their hiccups on us. Like my wife is easy to anger and I am easy to upset but hey we both balance each other that we don't need nor want anybody advice on us when all we need is God's advice! When I am wrong, I admit and apologize; when she is wrong she admits and apologizes now but before I can attest she would down herself and blame herself for her wrongs; she would punish herself when she did not need to do so. And you know, it was challenging to me because I didn't understand why but I knew it was familiar because I used to do it. I learned over time not to take everything to heart as if everything is my fault. I have expressed my past experiences with her and she has acknowledged and noticed some resemblance. For she has done the same and I too acknowledge and notice some similarities. I can say she has grown a lot within herself and our relationship. We both have. Don't get me wrong nor believe we are saints because we too have sinned and are aware of both of our faults whether it towards each other or those we have wronged or have said we wronged; we both own up to our actions, repented and asked for forgiveness. We cannot help who says what about our relationship or about us as individuals. These can come from those who have struggled to accept truth or do not want us to grow. I can say I do understand in a way that I will not hold anything against her but to help her realize when she has done something whether good bad or indifferent; and does the same for me also and I couldn't be anymore grateful to have someone who is willing to work in a relationship while seeking the guidance of God and still love me the same as our first date. You know it's crazy because some people will be in a relationship like it's the best and last but suddenly find themselves starting over. And it's funny, I used to have the mentality of starting over when it came to meeting someone for the first time. I say this because when I didn't have this mindset, I was confident and sure of this being something real; then reality would happen and God would show me otherwise of who they truly are. That's when I started to question myself and wonder what I am doing wrong; like I would think so bad about myself that I found myself wanting to be another person just so I can be happy. You see people will have you think they are interested and yet they are not because you don't possess certain qualities they like or have a certain look for their image. These things can make you feel as though you are not good enough to be with anyone; at least that's how I felt. Yet again, my God has proved to me that I am precious, that I am beautifully and wonderfully made, I am worthy to be a daughter, a sister, a mother, a friend to those who accept me and a wife to the one who loves me for me! No strings attached! By strings

I mean, there no other woman my wife would desire to have, there is no other mom my kids wish for, there's no other friend that would listen and actually care without jealous or envy, a sister who sticketh closer than any foe you call "sis", and a daughter who is loved and is appreciated by her Father who are above in heaven. I am more than enough. We all should believe and feel that we are more than what this world may label us to be let alone say who we are; We are children of God and when you are a child of God, you are more loved, more appreciated, more worthy and more than enough for him! Amen! I am grateful for my spouse and more grateful that God has given me the most unexpected relationship I couldn't ask for yet he gave it to me anyway. Thank you my Lord! Thank you!

So much to say. Where do I start? Well, what do you know about the meaning of dreams? Aside from what Google or Safari tells you, what do you know about dreams? Do you know how to interpret let alone have the discernment to understand what your dreams mean? You see, dreams are a mystery and I believe no human can truly interpret dreams unless God gives you the meaning. Not knocking any people who have made a career of this, get your money by any means. I believe, and this is me, I believe dreams can only be interpreted by God himself; for he knows what is to come before we even see the day coming. Like Joseph for example. You know the story of Joseph don't you? Not Mary's husband nor Jesus' earthly father Joseph. I am talking about a young boy named Joseph who loved God and favored by his father Israel amongst having seven other brothers; six being the eldests and one younger brother just a few years younger than Joseph. Joseph's father Israel loved his son so much that he made Joseph a coat of many colors, which made Joseph very happy but his older brothers very jealous and angry. Oh his brothers hated him and didn't want much to do with Joseph. One night Joseph had a dream and he expressed his dream to his father and brothers: Genesis 37:7 "For behold, we were binding sheaves in the field and lo, my sheaf arose, and also stood upright; and behold, your sheaves stood round about, and made obeisance to my sheaf". This truly made his brothers angry for their response was not of acceptance. They didn't like hearing Joseph speak of having authority over them! Then Joseph dreamed another dream and spoke unto his brothers and father, "Behold, I have dreamed a dream more and behold the sun and the moon and the eleven stars made obeisance to me". At this point Joseph's father spoke and rebuked all of his sayings yet he questioned Joseph about his dreams. Israel couldn't believe what Joseph was saying and believed he and his wife should only bow to the Lord thy God. But Joseph was not saying what his brothers and father had interpreted when he shared his dreams. To me, Joseph was expressing himself of what he believed was shown to him by God but he only got half of the story. He was only given the end of his life and not the middle for Joseph has lived knowing his beginning. What happened to Joseph next was unexpected. The day had come where Joseph brothers were out working in the field of Shechem feeding their father's flock. Israel had asked Joseph to go to the field of Shechem and see what thy brothers were up to and of course Joseph obeyed his fathers wishes. Now, Joseph knew at this point his older brothers did not care for him and even though he didn't want to go but out of the love for his father he went to see about his brothers anyway. As Joseph approached his destination, he met a man who was in the field where his brother's should have been who stated that Joseph 's brothers had gone to the land of Dothan. So Joseph rushed off to the land of Dothan and there he spotted his brothers; now his brothers saw Joseph coming from afar and did not want to be bothered with him. His brother's then began to plot, they started to converse amongst each other to slay Joseph. But one brother, Reuben, spoke up saying, "No, let us not kill him! Shed no blood but cast him into this pit that is in the wilderness and lay no hand upon him". The brothers agreed. They stripped Joseph of his beautiful colorful coat and cast him into the pit. Later that day, as the brothers were sitting around a fire eating bread, they noticed a company of Ishmeelites on their way from Gilead with a camel carrying an abundance of items for Egypt. Then once again, the brothers revisited the conversation of slaying Joseph and another brother, Judah, spoke saying " What profit is it if we slay our brother and carry his blood?" No response. Then Judah spoke again, "Come and let us sell him to the Ishmeelites and let not our hand be upon him; for he is our brother and our flesh". The other brothers agreed and Joseph was sold to the Ishmeelites for twenty pieces of silver. Can you imagine being sold for money by your own family?! I mean yes there are people being sold against their will across the world to those who do not care for them let alone themselves. Sad but it is true and will soon end. My God who hears all hurting hearts and tears of pain, deception, betrayal and fake love will put a stop to this here soon! Just believe, just pray, trust, keep your faith, stay strong within him and yourselves! Amen my Lord, I receive this for those who are too scared to claim it in Jesus name! Amen! Now, Joseph was sold and on his way to Egypt; his brothers had taken his coat, tore it up and covered it with blood from a baby goat whom they killed. The brothers went back to the land of Canaan and presented Joseph's torn bloody coat to their father, Jacob, stating Joseph had been killed by a wild beast. Jacob's heart was broken for he mourned his son for many days. Jacob, who was once named Israel but given the name Jacob by God, trying to be comforted by his sons and daughters but Jacob refused. As for Joseph he was sold again to a Potiphar, who was an officer of Pharaoh and captain of the guards. Joseph grew up to be an obedient servant not only to God but to his master whom he has served for many years. The master of the house saw God's favor over Joseph, he respected Joseph for his house was blessed because of Joseph. Joseph was pleased with his master and served him according to God's will, purpose and hand of grace; after many years Joseph was made overseer of his master's house. Soon after this, Joseph was thrown in jail because of the master's wife who falsely accused Joseph saying he was trying to force himself on her. The master of the house couldn't believe his ears but he loved his wife and had Joseph thrown in prison. Joseph spent many years in prison, the keeper of the prison knew the type of man Joseph is and committed Joseph to be in charge of the prisoners. God was with Joseph. He never left him nor forsake Joseph even in Joseph's darkest moments. Joseph gained a lot of respect from the prisoners and charge guards; he was well spoken of by those whom Joseph had come in contact with. Joseph also became known as a dream interpreter. He was placed in charge of two men thrown in prison by Pharoah, one was a butler and the other a baker. As a little time has passed, both the butler and the baker both had strange dreams but knew not what the dream meant. Both men were sent to Joseph for help; Joseph asked both men a question stating, " Do not interpretations belong to God?" then he asked them to tell him what they dreamed and the butler went first: " In my dream, a vine was before me and in the vine were three branches and though it was budded and blossoms; the clusters bring forth ripe grapes, the Pharaoh's cup was in my hand, I pressed the grapes into the Pharaoh's cup and placed the cup in his hand." Joseph responded, "Three branches mean in three days Pharaoh will lift his hand and you will be free and restore you to your post. But do think of me when the time comes and show kindness, speak of me to Pharaoh and bring me out of prison." When the baker saw that the butler received good interpretation, he went ahead and spoke to Joseph about his dream: " I also dreamed, I had three white baskets upon my head, the top basket was filled with all bakermeats for Pharaoh and the birds did eat from the basket on my head." Joseph responded, "Three baskets mean three days. In three days Pharaoh will lift his hand upon thee and will hang thee on a tree where birds will eat thy flesh off thee." So it was done as Joseph had interpreted the dreams of both the butler and the baker had come to pass. The butler was restored to his post as chief butler and handed the Pharaoh his cup; as for the baker he was hanged as said in Joseph's interpretation. The butler forgot about Joseph. He did not once bring Joseph's name to Pharaoh and was spoken upon him while in prison. Until two full years later, when Pharaoh dreamed a dream none of his council could make sense of his dreams, the butler then remembers Joseph. Pharaoh dreams were alarming to him because they came in a way that made him feel troubled. The butler spoke of Joseph and his kindness of how he interpreted his and the baker's dreams which both hath come to pass. Pharaoh sent word for Joseph, he was brought out of prison, he was shaved and given a change of clothes. Joseph was brought before Pharaoh who spoke of how he was having these dreams but no one could tell him the meaning of such dreams. Joseph informed Pharaoh that these interpretations do not come from him but from God who will give peace to the Pharaoh's mind. The Pharaoh told Joseph his dream, "I stood by a river bank, out of the river came seven kine fatfleshed well favoured and fed in a meadow; then I seen another seven kine come from the river behind the first seven kine but these were ill favoured and leanedfleshed and stood beside the other kine; then the ill favoured kine ate the other seven fatfleshed kine and I woke up. Then I dreamed a second time, there were seven ears of corn in one stalk good and full; another seven ears all withered, thin and blasted the east wind and sprung up after the first seven good ears; then the thin ears devoured the seven good ears." Joseph responded, "The dream of Pharaoh is God has shown Pharaoh what is to come in the land of Egypt; the seven good ears are seven years of good and plentiful of food; and the seven ill favoured kin which came after and the seven empty ears blasted with the east wind are seven years of famine and great wave of grief. Since Pharaoh has dreamed twice then it shall come to pass by God." I am sure the Pharaoh was in shock and some disarray but Joseph knew what Pharaoh must do. Joseph advised Pharaoh to appoint officers to ensure there is enough food to last those seven years of famine; let those keep food in the cities, store food so the land of Egypt does not perish from famine. Pharaoh saw Joseph's vision and agreed. Joseph was placed in charge of men who stored food and Pharaoh had given Joseph his ring as a symbol of trust and authority. Joseph was given the finest clothing and chain upon his neck; he was also given chariots and a wife whom he soon came to love. Joseph was only thirty years old when he stood before Pharaoh. The first seven years were plentiful and good; the cities were filled with food. Joseph gathered as much food like the sand of the sea and when the next seven years drew near when the first seven gave plenty; As Egypt had become touched with famine, the people cried to Pharaoh though he directed them to see Joseph. When famine was in the midst, Joseph opened all storehouses and gave food to those in need. Little did Joseph know he would soon come face to face with his past. Famine had reached the land of Canaan where Joseph was born and partially raised yet sold by his brothers at a young age. At this time Joseph is governor over all the land; his brethren had come to buy food for their father had sent them. Joseph recognized his brothers but they knew Joseph not for they bowed low to the earth and did not look to him. Joseph remembered his dream from whence he was younger but then called his brothers spies. Why? I have no idea, maybe he was pranking them idk. His brethren denied all accusations stating "they are only son's of one man in the land of Canaan who has twelve sons; one of the youngest are with their father and the other is not". Joseph then tested his brothers and asked them to bring forth the youngest child in three days' time while one of them stayed in prison until the rest returned with their youngest brother. Joseph's brothers begged, pleading with him to not ask for such a request for they knew this would break their fathers heart more than what has been done. Still the brothers knew not it was Joseph standing before them until...on the third day the brothers returned with their youngest brother Benjamin; Simeon who was left behind in prison was released to dine with them and Joseph for a feast. They had a good time it seemed, Joseph composed himself despite what he was truly feeling. The day had come for his brothers to return to the land of Canaan to be with their father. Joseph had given them plenty of food and money in their sacks. Then he put his brethren to one last test and that was the test of "truth and loyalty". Joseph had commanded one of his servants to place a silver cup in the youngest brother's sack. Joseph then sent his steward after his brothers after they had cleared the city; and when they came upon them the brothers, they were searched and found the silver cup in Benjamin's sack and they were brought back to Joseph's house. When Joseph saw the cup was in Benjamin's sack he commanded for him to be his servant. The brothers begged and pleaded with Joseph to not do this for he is the only child left of his mother whom their father loved most! The brother's then confessed if they were to return without Benjamin, their father would surely die for they had already lost one brother and could not bare to lose another and their father also. Joseph saw the compassion, honesty and regret in his brother's eyes, he then began to cry. He cried out loud the land of Egypt and the house of Pharaoh heard Joseph's cry. Joseph then revealed himself to his brothers who could not believe that their younger brother was alive and lord over all of Egypt. Joseph spoke saying, "This was God's plan, for he sent me before you to preserve the land of Egypt. He sent me to help save lives and deliver all from the famine that has come before us! Come to me my brothers, for I am Joseph. Go to my father and tell him his son Joseph lives and ye all come and stay with me in the land of Goshen." Joseph and his brethren wept and rejoiced together. Pharaoh commanded for wagons to be brought forth for Joseph's father to come to stay. Jacob was reunited with his son, Joseph, whom he thought was dead; his spirit was revived and Jacob was able to see his son again before he died. How happy they all were in the end compared to how things started.

Now you can see the interpretation of a dream can come off bad to those whose ears are not open but good in the end for those whose heart is not closed yet filled with faith, belief and trust in God. All can be well according to his will, glory and purpose. Amen God! We thank you for the lesson in which Joseph has experienced but was shared for us to learn. Those who have yet to grasp the concept of your word, we pray to you to open their minds and fill their hearts with your understanding. I thank you for not only my life lessons but for the lessons displayed in your word today as well as yesterday and so forth. Please heavenly father continue to watch over us all as we venture through the dark shadows of this world. For we walk by faith and not by sight because our faith is your eyes dear Lord and our steps are your words. Amen!

Dream Moment

Why do people act the way they do? Why use a weapon when a person only have their hands or words to plead and defend themselves? Honestly, those who use weapons as a form of power and demand are true cowards at heart. Even though words do have power it is simply not enough for them to "get what they want and/or desire". They seek first to draw an object to cause harm rather than draw hands to pray and seek God's help. A weapon is seen as "life empowering" when really it's "life deceiving". For God is the word and his word is empowering when believed. Words are most powerful and can manifest the most righteous according to God's will, purpose and for all his glory. Most will not understand let alone believe what is said but look at our world today. Many live in fear because they do not understand how and why this "pandemic" is happening or even what brought it about to this entire world. Most countries, states and cities have moved on with faith not dwelling on what is constantly being spoken about. The words that circle our nation's news are of untruth for the truth "if" revealed will be chaotic and may cause distrust within our country. According to these theories, those who seek God now due to what is known as "man's mistake", should have been seeking God before this "pandemic" has started. For this is like the time of Egypt when many Egyptians did not know of God but heard about him through Moses asking Pharaoh to let God's people go and yet Pharaoh denied these requests multiple times; then God began his reign of plaques among Pharaoh and Egypt to show he has true power not what man created themselves to prove this was a big hoax. Until the last plague took the lives of every firstborn son including Pharaoh one and only son; hardened his heart and he let God's people go. God's words, his promises carry a long way for us to believe and trust him with all our hearts but lean unto his understanding of life. Those who push God's word upon those who know him not are the ones who are afraid of death and know him not as he has known us; ye may love him with thine mouth confession but still showeth fear, doubt and untrust in thine hearts. To walk through a door, then try to climb through a window to come back from where you once left is a bit redundant don't you agree? Yes, you can factor many scenarios for this but how can any of them fit your relationship with God? You walked away from him and shut the door because you no longer believed let alone had trust in what he has instore for your life; so you shut the door and go handle life on your own but then life takes an unexpected turn you come back through a window which you cannot climb or enter without seeking forgiveness but you beg for mercy while still trying to climb. That shows determination but it doesn't faith; that shows persistence but it doesn't show trust; that shows conditional love but it doesn't show respect for the love God has already given you over and over and over again. So again, how does that work? You know God has placed you on a path he made for you and you decide to walk away because it wasn't a path according to how and what you wanted let alone desired; it wasn't an easy life for you. God is worthy of trust, love, loyalty and honor but here we are being ungrateful while seeking mercy on every bad moment we have! We have nothing to lose except what is lost already, nothing to worry about except what you have worried about already; he has worked it out people! Amen, I pray ye have found the strength, the faith, the courage and the trust to walk on the path God has laid before them. For we may do his will, know to trust his purpose and know all is for his glory but is for our own good.

This may seem to be uneasy and uncertain but comforting as he guides us "hands on" to who he wants us to be; what he needs us to see and where he provided us to stay. Any path God places you on will be uneasy and feel uncomfortable because God only comforts our hearts in every step we shall take and knowing within our spirit that he will never leave nor forsake us! It may feel like it but know he is all around us even though we may not be able to physically see him or touch him, he is present right before us and dwells within our hearts. Believe, trust and have continuous faith no matter what this world may say, do or even take! God is with us all, Amen!

Dream Moment End

I've had many conversations, some which have helped others while many have become offended. Often these conversations are deep which can be related to what's going on in the world or become very personal to which I hardly ever ask it just seems to happen. A lot of these conversations resort to home life, like relationships or children or children and relationships together. Mind you I am no expert in either one of those topics, I am learning just like the rest of us but I do speak on any experiences I may or may not have encountered in my life. I can say this, for I believe any or whatever it is that goes on in your home should only be discussed with those in the home. Now it's ok to seek advice from those you trust will not steer you wrong. However, be sure to know whatever answer or advice you seek is what you originally have decided before you asked that person for their advice. Truth be told, telling those outside of your home about what's going on is more of a "gossip" starter for them because you may or may not know what they are going through despite what they tell you. You see, many people will say they are an open book when really they are closed and will leave out certain details of their life because they might find it embarrassing or not good enough to the person whom they are speaking to about it. Especially when it comes to those who are in a relationship whether it's marriage, or engaged or simply just boyfriend/girlfriend or boyfriend/boyfriend or girlfriend/girlfriend. No matter the life or relationship you have, all advice is not always good advice. Now this may ruffle a few feathers or even cause more wrinkles than needed from scrounging faces: but when seeking advice from a human point of view instead of God's view can be a bit messy. Meaning you may think you're getting the help you need for a situation but really you're just giving this person something to talk about with another person who may or may not like you and probably doesn't want the best for you. Now I can be wrong but it has been proven especially when inadvertently brought to the other person's attention. Again, I may be wrong but please be careful of who you tell your life to. Their advice may not be the advice you would want to go off because in my experience it can lead to resentment with whoever you may have a problem with. So, why not seek God's advice and/or comfort? People seek advice from other people because they can see and touch them, meaning get some form of "sympathy" from them opposed to what they can get from God. It's the "physical comfort" I like to call it. When a person cries and/or upset you can get a hug from another person or a "pat" on the shoulders; you know that "there there" gesture most people do lol. And we do this because we truly believe that this person has experienced this before or may know what we should do next. And yet, is God not capable of doing such things also? As crazy as it may seem but with this there do be consequences especially if we were to do what another person says instead of what God wants us to do in the first place. I can speak from experience because I have gone to people who I believed loved and supported my life because of who I was with but really they only wanted me to be like them: alone. I say this because those who I spoke to about my relationship were actual single ladies with some "hurt/relationship" issues. I mean when I felt as if I was in the darkest moments of my relationship, while seeking God's advice I also sought the advice of others I could see and touch for their advice and all I received in return was "Well, may you need just leave her alone and find somebody else" "see she just like all the other niggas too" or "Maybe you should just be by yourself, live alone just you and the kids and let the universe bring whoever into your life to be with. Just leave that alone"; But couldn't look me in the eye while saying these things to me. And you know, that's my mistake, that's my fault for even speaking to them in the first place! Did I know yes but still giving the benefit of the doubt and because they have had previous relationships and this being my first; I thought they could help. And yet my thought has led me to negativity and nothing positive. I should've patiently waited for God's response and guidance; which I did! And we are still together till this day because the Lord has guided me, corrected both of us in our wrongs and showed us that he wanted for us despite what other people were saying! And you know it wasn't just me who experienced this, my wife did too and she was like "what the hell" and was in disbelief just how I was. You know what's funny let alone ironic about all this, those who spoke these things about our relationship in the beginning are no longer in our lives. They're still living, alive and well but my wife and I don't associate with them anymore and it wasn't our choice they just simply faded away from our path. You see, God will show you who's for you and who's not for him. He will let you live life as though you thought but will show you the intermission. For we continued to pray and seek God's advice and not listen to others. Wow! God is good! He is amazing and can do more than those who say "they mean no harm" but causes the most damage! God is extraordinary, he is a wonder, he is a wise counselor, a teacher and most of all a Father to the fatherless! Thank you Lord for all you have done! You heard my cry, you heard my pain, you saw my need for help. You came through, gave me the comfort I deserved but I felt undeserving yet you showed up and showed out by delivering those who say were for me but naturally against me! God your timing is perfect and your purpose rectified our situation and made us stronger than before! Wow, amen amen and amen!

Now most people will become upset with God. They become upset or angry or both when God does not appear when they ask him right in that specific moment. And the moment can be of many things like illness, broken heartedness or even death. Most people feel God is being cruel or unforgiving when they experience things like those listed above but ultimately he is just letting life run its course. I know very few people who say they have been given second chances at life and praise God for letting them see another day(s). Then there are many who turn their noses up because someone they thought didn't deserve to get sick or even die to be gone but they are. And that's based on what they knew of that person. See again, people will only show/tell you about their lives because they don't want you to think the worst or bad of them especially when they know it about themselves. While you are upset with God over whatever you thought he did, why not praise him for what he does do that benefits your likings, your needs and wants? Don't get it twisted now, God does supply all needs according to his will, his purpose and guess what…his timing! But not when we ask him to nor expect him to deliver on a silver platter right then and there. And what's sickening, people will be so quick to praise for "blessings" but not praise him for the loss of a loved one who God has planned for them in his kingdom. Ever thought of it that way? Or possibly God foresaw what that person would do to themselves or another person who didn't deserve but is going to do it anyway then retaliation would cause more pain and suffering that is not necessary. Have you ever thought maybe this person didn't want to live anymore or maybe this person's illness could save the lives of many due to a cure created from that person's blood? I mean we were all cured, we were saved through Jesus Christ blood. And this was before any of us were a twinkle in daddy's eye or warmth in our mother's undies. How many have ever received an unexpected blessing and paid it forward to bless another who doesn't know what a blessing is? I'm not talking about tithing or you see someone on the street and give them some change or a couple bucks. I mean really pay it forward on a higher level of where you are today? Show of hands. I can say I have not paid it forward on a higher level than I am today but I have done things for those who didn't have much but needed my help and didn't even ask. I have encountered those who are at grocery stores with minimal food yet have this big cart full and let them go before me regardless of it being one or two people I still let them go. I do pray one day I can pay it forward on a higher level than where I am today. I do pray God will be like "Help them." and it be clear as day no matter what I am doing or where I may be in a hurry to; I will do my Lord's will and help them. And there are many people out here on the streets who do have the credibility to work but choose not too. They would rather be on the streets than to help themselves get off the streets. And there is a job hiring right where they are panhandling. It's like enabling a behavior for children who have dreams to change the world but their parents are showing them otherwise. I get that you don't have to tell your children to do as you do and they can be whoever they want when they grow up but what solid feedback can you give them when they are actually out in this world trying to make the difference they once dreamed but all they can remember is their parents being on the streets begging for help. Let alone seeing their mom or dad or both struggle to keep not only food on the table but a roof over their heads and clothes on their backs. What do you say? I apologize if this offends many nor am I judging anyone. I'm just curious on what you would tell your child once adulthood comes about. I do pray and hope God does help you all in this time of change. And trust this world is going to change in a way any of us including the government least expects it. This I pray, just prepare yourself, prepare your hearts, your minds and get your spirits ready; for he's coming! As one of the online pastors of Elevation Church would say, "Stop crying, it's coming!"; Stop crying, stop worrying, stop doubting and start believing, start trusting God, have crazy faith and pray for better! I know giving to those in need is a bit much and many of you have your own thoughts and opinions about this; but think of this and tell your response to God: "If you were given ten or even a hundred million dollars, God instructed you to help those on the street began a fresh start, would you give until all within your neighborhood is helped or would you only give to a few and keep the rest for yourself"? Now, I do understand having this much money could put a target on your back or even bring forth dishonest people or even people in your life who will try to persuade you otherwise with their hidden intentions. Just know no matter what you decide it will be more than enough especially when you listen to that inner voice which is soft and overshadowed by many other voices but still you will hear it clear as day. My question is, will you listen or will you ignore it? My response to this question, and this is my honest answer: "If this be my Lord will then let his will be done! For he has given me the answer to a question I asked many moons ago and he brought forth the day for those who have cried for his help, he is sending thy faithful servant to help his people in need. Therefore, I am available to the Lord my God and see that his will be done!" Now again, don't get this twisted meaning, I will know who is true and who is false; I will know who will take this out of content to gain for their own personal needs and those who are under the Lord's covenant and have been blessed with this reading. So if I were you, please think and pray twice before trying to humiliate yourself in God's eye. God bless.

Faithful Rogue:

Are you aware of what true faith is? Please, do not give me: Hebrews 11:1 " Now faith is the substance of things hoped for, the evidence of things not seen." this is not what I am asking. Do you know what true faith is? True faith is the evidence of things not seen yet are hoped for though the substance can be of many things. True faith comes from waiting before, during and after prayer made, endured, and received. You know what grinds my gears, is how we can be so quick to throw scriptures and interpretations on today's society and yet not a soul has dared to ask God if this is what he truly desires of us. Yea, most will give themselves to God but pick themselves back up as though they can work on themselves better than God. The moment God gave his word, created man: man took and ran what he got out of it and not what God truly meant. To be a help. Be fruitful, multiply, replenish the earth yes but subdue it. And yet we cannot love one another as he has loved us, for we were not created to be the same but different and peculiar people. Not shaming nor condemning; for this is not my place nor why I am present. I am just speaking the obvious. If spirits are alike in groups then there can be no difference; but if spirits are different then they cannot be alike and will be outcasted. Listen, I am no woman of importance but I am the daughter of one who gives me the words to speak; and for him I shall honor and glorify always. Yea my walk is different from thou but still I worship thee, my Lord, in the dark as well as the noonday all day. None may understand my word and yet I love God, I love Jesus and I love you all! God bless.

              Faithful Rogue End

  The heart suffers most, for it feels more than the mind can think. Faith is a substance of things hope for the evidence of things not seen. My heart hopes for what is not seen opposed to what my mind sees through ears and eyes alike. Waking nights, I cry and cry then pray and pray while crying and praying all at the same time. I ask my heavenly Father for the faith I seek to be revealed unto me yet it remains in the midst of his mysterious wonders. The feeling of those terrified, hurt and lost for those who seek with their minds seek with their eyes and ears but not with their hearts tears flow down my face. My Lord, my God please bring me together as one, though I feel separated by many. Tears flow as my faith goes deeper within thee to the core of thy spirit which lies within me. Not many will understand this but most shall feel what is being said within. My Lord, please walk with me as I desire to walk with you; guide me through the shadows of death as I fear none worse than evil. Release those who are not of thy covenant, let them see your glorious light shine through their darkest moments! My Father, who art in heaven, as thee hour approaches I appreciate, love and want more of you! Revelation, your victory is here with a sign of judgment on arms. Please Lord, have great mercy upon those who know not, who believe otherwise of you as you are who you say you are. I beg, I plead with thee not only my testimony but my heart I give only to you for you deserve all of me and more! The power of self-giving, the power of honesty, love; the power of faith unwavered stand still within the holy spirit is most undesirable but gracious and wonderful. Mercy to all, blessings to many and faith towards those who have not within; let God's will serve his purpose for it is for the good of mankind alike! His glory lives on, his victory is forever Amen!

What do you seek when you walk? What do you seek when you drive? Outside of your surroundings and paying attention to the road; is there something your spirit looks for while you are outside your home? It's strange because I feel so much sadness and yet have so much to be grateful for. Hard to explain as tears unfold suddenly but I do not know why I feel this way or why the tears come unexpectedly. If I were to explain, well try to explain to someone who I know or do not know; I would be told simply I am not happy and I am afraid. Which is not true but can hold some truth. I am happy but I do get sad from time to time just like most people in this world. Writing makes me feel at ease and I am free to express myself without critics or the opinions of others who feel as if I should keep my thoughts within. I know my speaking is blunt but it is the honesty that makes it what it is and not everyone can handle honesty nowadays without some sort of retaliation or harsh consequences. I love the life I live but have moments where I cry for reasons to none. I believe my tears are for those who say they live peacefully by mouth but are in complete chaos. My opinion of course but you must know my faith has been taken on many roads where I have seen what I did not expect to see. I have walked and still walk blindly with God as my guide, for he is my feet and guides me to where he wants me to be. No questions asked but we all ask questions to what we do not understand and would like understanding. Now, I've had my moments of regrets to which I can admit but have also forgiven myself for those moments and not be too hard on myself. I know God knows who I am nor does he be harsh on me but simply redirects me to where I should be going. I know not to dwell or feed on those who give negative thoughts and/or feelings; their opinions about me and my life. I believe there are certain lessons in life that will teach you to be humble, to have gratitude and respect; to be aware of the mercy that has been given by God. Spiritually I am sickened by the force that lies ahead and yet I am steadfast in faith, shielded with God's word and know his presence is all around me! You know there are talks that go round and round. How do I stay in this "toxicity" inhaling what has no real form of truth? How do I keep going day to day knowing the temptations of the world are purely out of control? To blame one on another for one cannot accept truth nor admit their wrongs. For it is simple, the answer is this purpose is not mine, it is the Lord God's and his will shall be done and victory shall be praised; joy shall be counted to the utmost high our God! Ephesians 3:19-21 says, "And to know the love of Christ, which passeth knowledge, that ye might be filled with all the fullness of God. Now unto him that is able to do exceedingly abundantly above all that we ask or think, according to the power that worketh in us, Unto him be the glory in the church by Christ Jesus throughout all ages, world without end. Amen". Moment of truth and how they twist by those who only understand in comfortability to them. The matters of how people may feel regarding the preaching of God's word or even teaching to those who do not understand his word; lies within the battle of their truth and God's truth. Man will follow the word of God and make it their own understanding and not God's true understanding. I have noticed, well heard there were questions regarding women having the anointing to preach let alone teach God's word to the world. All of this came about from what was scripted by the Apostle Paul in 1 Timothy 2:9-15, "In like manner also, that women adorn themselves in modest apparel, with shamefacedness and sobriety; not with braided hair, or gold, or pearls, or costly array; But (which becometh women professing godliness) with good works. Let the women learn in silence with all subjection. But I suffer not a woman to teach, nor usurp authority over the man, but to be in silence. For Adam was first formed, then Eve. And Adam was not deceived, but the woman being deceived was in transgression. Notwithstanding she shall be saved in childbearing, if they continue in faith and charity and holiness with sobriety". The meaning of these scriptures have been revised on more than one paper. Of course being written by man who God trusted his word to be his word unrevised by anyone. It's like "he said what he said" so don't add what is not necessary or spoken to be true when it is not. I honestly believe Paul was not trying to discredit woman's ability to do what man can do; for even then he only knew what was of his time not the time that has now come. Meaning he did not know the truth of what the world would be like now opposed to what it was back then. However in today's world women have come a long way and have found favor in God. I believe Paul was trying to spare women from hardships and humility that man would lay before them if they were to try and do what man is doing. For man will be ashamed of woman to be called to do God's purpose and to carry out his will in a way man can not. God created woman to be a help to man, to grow beside him and not have authority over him but too share the authority with him. To show man what he fails to see or has not felt due to his masculinity, but to show him there is a different way than a "macho" way. I believe Paul was saying even though women give birth to a child but she can also birth something new to the world man has no capability of doing. Even though a woman was deceived before does not mean she is bound to be deceived forever! Anyone who believes God can use a virgin woman to birth his only begotten son, whom shall ever live died on the cross for all sins then and now; shall believe he has found favor in woman to preach and teach his word. For women have learned in silence long enough! Now is the time for women to rise and stand with men not against him as he so forth thinks let alone believe. Women have carried the word of God not only in their womb but within their hearts growing into their spirit. Yes God, Amen! For women are blessed just as much as men yet have found more favor in God and Jesus Christ our Savior because of their faith, their trust in him to see us through all that is good, bad and indifferent. Man has spoken of faith and trust with thine mouths yet showeth fear in their actions which they need to be held accountable just as women have and are. For Jesus can help with what is most troubling and what is most deceiving. Let us all work together and not against one another. All genders alike be merciful and grateful knowing we are loved and yet bleed the same as our Lord Jesus Christ, Amen? God bless.

    I have had many thoughts as well as dreams and often wonder, "Why am I having these thoughts, these dreams which make no sense but make sense consciously?" Subconscious wise, it is clear of what lingers in the back there where it's no sense to be made. Lately I have been seeing numbers, numbers of sequences which at this time I do not know what it means but knew deep down what they are meant. You know how at times you understand yet somehow confuse yourself and then be like, "God why?" lol. Yea well, that's me! Of course my Lord God knows I mean no harm nor question his will but he also knows I am of a curious mind as well as soul. When seeing these numbers in sequence and by sequence I mean, "444, 666, 222, 333, 777, 555"; those sequences and so forth. And of course some to many of these are very meaningful spiritually and also forms of manifestation. If you were to ask Dr. Google or any other person who studies numbers will give their "researched" interpretations but will it give you let alone satisfy your curiosity you are feeling deep within. Like it will satisfy the mind but not ease what is troubling within nor fulfill the empty bucket of answers needed for these questions if that makes sense. I have asked God for his revelation on what these sequence numbers mean and how does it involves me or evolves me. I say evolves because what has been revealed to me most recently is that God is with me always even when I feel as though I am alone. Also that my ancestors are at peace knowing their generations are not holding on to curses that plagued them once or twice before. And to know it is ok to break what is known as "generational curses" is a good thing! No one should feel as if they are bringing shame or disappointing anybody especially if you yourself are not happy and are hurting deeply. Never feel as if you are or will be the blame especially when freeing yourself from past encounters that carried on into your present. Do not wait until a loved one is gone to try to free yourself especially when they are part of your healing! Remember, no one is perfect, no one is incapable of making mistakes; we are all learning parents and childrens alike! But also know parents were children once and children will be parents soon; believe you can change what was instilled in you as if it is you but really someone else and change to who God has already instilled in you before you were born. Free yourself! I remember seeing "666" for a number of days straight. Like three days straight and it was alarming at first because growing up I was told "666" was a bad omen, it was the sign of the Devil and no good was to come. Until I asked God, "Lord, what does this number mean and why am I seeing this consecutively?" So, as the next day rose, I saw the same numbers "666" twice and then when I thought I saw it for a third time it wasn't, it showed "6111". Then a voice spoke from within stating, "you can Google or you can believe no harm will come from seeing these numbers and know I am with you always". Instantly I had chills and thought I was freezing! But knowing it wasn't cold outside and my heavenly Father was all around me was a true blessing, rejoiceful feeling to endure. And I thank him all the days of my life for his word. You may not believe and most will Google to see the meaning of sequence numbers but none of those interpretations will amount to the revelation of God himself! Amen! Thank you Lord you are here, there all around front and back; side to side! Thank you! For he surrounds us all even when you don't see him but know he is around! Hallelujah! I remember a woman, a close friend who was at her breaking point, ready to give up on it all. I said Lord, I don't know what to say or to do for her except come to you! All I could say to her was,

"Please, do not give up, you must carry on, pray and fight for the life that is laid before you! It may look like brown grass and muddy dirt patches but it is all for his glory you must believe and mostly keep faith!" Her tears so real, her heart pouring out loud but I knew God was listening, he could hear her and was closer than she thought. Whoa those chills, I tell ya! We finished our talk and she went home. The next day she came to work feeling a lot better. She said it was like a weight lifted off her shoulders and heart was relieved. All I could say is "Amen" and thank God for being with her! Till this day her faith remains strong and her trust in him is stronger than it was before. She is now walking in her path God has laid before her and has accepted him and knows Jesus Christ is her Lord and Savior. Amen! How beautiful is life to know God is the outcome of every situation we may find dark and lonely? It is mighty gorgeous if you ask me! The glory, the honor our Lord deserves on more than one occasion; praising his name out loud and deep within. Jesus, Jesus, Jesus! Say it loud and proud; and hold on to his truth within your hearts. Spiritual warfare is near, almost coming once again for the Lord lives beyond the hills as we lift our eyes high and beyond. We look for him, which our help cometh from all praise, glory and honor and even giving ourselves is more than enough! Peace, amen!

I feel like crying. I am not sure why Lord but I do feel like crying. The purpose of my tears are of course for you will and glory my Lord but still the pain is of many others than my own. Have you ever had one of those nights where you're just sitting or lying there and tears start to flow? These moments are most precious and appreciated because you know you are in the presence of God. The chills are so real they are presumed as "freezing" but the holy spirit is not to make you comfortable but aware of his presence. Therefore his presence is uncomfortable so you know it is God that is with you for he has chosen you for a reason hence why he is in the room. Many may disagree with this and say, " well it is winter and cold outside so maybe your he is not working right or the heat needs to be turned up or it's too cold take the AC out the window". So many assumptions can go with what was said but none will be of truth. I love God and Jesus Christ our Savior wholeheartedly! I am thankful to be God's daughter and a fellow sister to Christ Jesus. Although it has been said God has no grandchildren, only children. However, I appreciate God and Jesus both for all the teaching, the lessons I have learned over my life and still learning; all love shown upon me and my family I'm just so beyond grateful! Yes there is so much going on in this world today with "he said she said, the government said" that I know within my heart God will overcome the sadness, wickedness and judgments there is! Jesus Christ will prevail and rule over all who has doubted, showeth lies upon God's word, given corruption and death! God's hand is over all and Jesus will show his face when least expected no science nor evangelist can predict this nor give accuracy. Even though the world is not ready but must be ready therefore we all have no choice but to bow. People will feel as though Christ and God alone are not understanding and will judge them for their flesh but he has been so merciful and yet we have taken his mercy for granted. Therefore he will judge us all according to his

Father's word. And the crazy thing about this is, God holds no grudge and Jesus carries no revenge so why assume what judgment is? For God is the kingdom and his son Jesus holds all power, glory and victory forever Amen!

    To be honest, I have a sinful mind yet I am forgiven but only in hope. I pray that I may be or truly are forgiven by God himself. Giver of eternal life yet ruler of the damned alike; I pray I am amongst those forgiven through Jesus Christ whose blood was shed on Calvary many many centuries ago. I know, well I believe in my heart that we are all forgiven of our sins even before we knew what sins would be before we were born. Though we are born into sin, we tend to be put on sin as though we knew what it was from the womb. Truthfully no man can prove a baby is of sin without the child first having sight let alone walking in life. Whether one mind says otherwise, while mouths plead the fifth amendment and actions speaks the truth of their heart. However, the question which wonders if Jesus died only to forgive sins of theft, murder, adultery, and those who lie for shame to honor not both thy mother and father; and to have children out of marriage or even disobey God's word he has written to keep order in the land which he created. Hmm, makes you rethink what was and what truth really is. Though I pray for clarity, God's true revelation on what should be still I believe in my heart Jesus died for many sins which have and have not yet come to life! Regardless of who you are within this life, the only important question is do you believe Jesus is life and death? Do you believe Jesus died to save you before you even met you; before you knew who you were until you seen it for yourself? It doesn't matter what the world sees you, what matters is how God saw your true self before the world labeled you! Have you seen you? Have you met your true self? Better yet, have you met your true self before or after the world labeled who you are in their eyes versus God's eyes? I'll wait. God loves us all the same! Whether you're a man out sleeping with many women or a woman out sleeping with many men; whether you're with a man/man or woman/woman God still loves you all the same! God doesn't just change, he evolves! God can evolve to so many levels no elevator can reach. God can go higher than any building built. NO man can touch him! For Jesus sits on the right hand on him! Family, we are all loved the same yet we are different from one another, peculiar in a way only God understands. Listen, John 9:1-11 there was a man who has been blind since birth and as Jesus passed by he saw this man. His disciples asked, "Master, who did sin, this man, or his parents, that he was born blind?" Jesus answered " Neither hath this man sinned, nor his parents: but that the works of God should be made manifest in him." I'm a pause and ask you: What sins have those of the same sex committed for ye to "rightfully judge"? If neither parent sinned, nor the person in question sinned, they were just born this way, then why are you taking it upon yourselves to judge a life where God's work is to be manifested in them? Why interfere in God's work? Why interfere with his plans because it doesn't agree with yours? So many will disagree, most will protest their anger and others will simply say "thank you Lord!". We should not, we shall not assume what it is God expects us to be nor should we assume what his word is instructing us! We are not God nor are we his apprentice nor first mate on this boat. We are his children and we must keep that in mind and stop trying to speak for him when God can speak for himself. Let us not judge for this is not our place and we will soon be in a space where Jesus' presence will speak louder than any defense mechanism you can "try" to come up with but will not stand. Have true faith, real belief, real love, honor and obedience! Know the presence of Christ is upon us all and he will judge according to his Father. Let us bow not only with our heads but our knees showing our gratitude, our gratefulness and our hearts say "Amen", "Yes, Lord", while our spirits praise and sing joys of righteousness! Peace of many blessings and when mercy shows know it is upon us all! God bless family!

For those who may feel as though they need to see or touch in order to believe there is a God...are more blind than a man who was born with no sight. For a man who is born with no sight has more faith than a man who was born with sight and far more belief than man who was born to hear or speak than a man who was not. John 9:39-41 " And Jesus said, For judgment I am come into this world, what they which see not might see; and that they which see might be made blind. And some of the Pharisees which were with him heard these words, and said unto him, Are we blind also? Jesus said unto them, If ye were blind, ye should have no sin: but now ye say, We see; therefore your sin remaineth." One who believes, truly, shall see. One who lies of sight, is truly blind. Prior to these scriptures, Jesus had just given a man his sight who has been blind since birth. There is such a commotion about it because those who have known this man could not understand how it that he sees for they believed his blindness was due to sin. They questioned the man, people around him and even his parents. The answers given were just not enough for the people so Jesus presents himself to the man because he was casted out from those who believed him not. As Jesus speaks to the man, then the Pharisees who are near Jesus and the man begin to ask questions even though they are not accepting of his answer. So not many people were accepting of his presence, even the man who was blind- when Jesus asked him "Dost thou believe on the Son of God?" And the man was honest saying, "Who is he, Lord, that I might believe on him?" And Jesus reveals himself to this man stating " Thou hast both seen him, and it is he that talketh with thee." And the man said " I believe" and he worshiped him on the spot. I mean the gratitude for the gift that was given. I believe, when Jesus does come, not many people will be accepting but expecting. I say this because back then people had a hard time accepting but did not expect the miracles Jesus has bestowed upon them. For today's society, and having spent the years of temptation, I believe people will not be accepting of Christ but expecting him to do the impossible so they may continue another thousand years of temptation. No ma'am, no ham no turkey! Those who feel as though they are obligated will push themselves forth to be in his presence yet are seen like Pharisees only wanting more than their minds can fathom. You cannot captivate Christ for he is not easy to hold nor is he anyone's prisoner. You have not his permission! Christ is our Savior, he is our Lord like no other you can make nor imagine! I do pray for when Jesus returns it will not be like before nor will it be worse then before but gracious and more merciful than today. I pray when Christ comes, people will be more open and aware, not closed off and not expect him to perform miracles on healing. For this will be ashamed to deceive Christ in his face as though his life on Calvary meant nothing yet your life does. All lives matter regardless of color, gender or body index; all lives matter! There's no forgive me, spare me and I'll praise your name for five seconds, possibly a minute with one cheek and then back to basic with the other cheek. Try and ye shall fail. Keep his truth, believe in his word always; not for personal gain or to be better than the next person. Expect nothing from Christ. He will perceive your thoughts before you can speak it. Keep God's word, know his truth, ask for his guidance and believe in faith! Christ is playing no games upon arrival, this I can say with confidence. Lord, I pray you are as merciful now as you were then; for ye has been merciful yet we have taken thee for granted. Please forgive those who are blind but see only what they want to see. I pray for those who are blind yet their faith and trust is stronger than many who wavers from time to time. I pray for those who cannot hear but have an ear for you Lord. Even me Lord, I waver from time to time yet I hold strong your word with faith which lies deep within my spirit! Thank you Lord, for evolving, for being everlasting, gracious, loving and forgiving! Thank you! God bless.

Regardless of how I feel not only about myself and other people, I thank God for every moment given, for every help he provides so I can overcome obstacles that are greater both seen and unseen. I am grateful to have learned so much and still learning till this very day, this very moment. I thank him for my mistakes because without them I would have learned nothing nor have grown into this amazing woman/wife/mother he is calling me to be! No matter what anyone has to say about me really doesn't matter because it's their opinion and everyone is entitled to their opinion. The only one who matter to me most is God. I am more so grateful for God's guidance through times which to me were dark and unbearable but to him full of light and blessings. We learn more and more about life as we live and will never stop learning! Everyday to every moment is a lesson learned whether you recognize it or not; whether you believe it or you're just too naive to see it! We are all accountable for the actions we take and the decisions we make. You will learn more and more until the Lord says it's time to come home. Even so when that happens, will he say "Well done, my faithful servant" or send thee to the everlasting pit. Like how remarkable is that yet terrifying?! Look, we can't change the past, we can only learn from it, own up to it and be prepared for what life unexpectedly throws your way. What we can do is thank God for every eye opening day, every moment of breathe taken in the fresh air, every "it's good to see you even though you don't like me but I love you anyway have a blessed day"; Just thank God for the little things like the sun shining bright or the moon glowing, the stars beaming and the wind churring breezes here and there! Just be grateful, for tomorrow is not promised to any of us! You can go to bed with the next day planned yet wake up to something totally different than what you originally planned and that my friend is the hardest pill to swallow. And what's even harder to accept that you'll never converse, hug, or kiss the person you love most and the same will be for them. There was a time, such as now, when I always planned for the next day and the day after and so forth. Which really gave me such anxiety that it became rough to sleep. To my wife who reminded me of the Israelites were in the wilderness and they were crying out about not having any food; so Moses prayed and God delivered manna and said for them to get only enough for the day and for their household. But the people were greedy and stored up enough not just for the day but for the next day also. When the next day came, the manna had spoiled and once again the Isrealites were out of food and crying out again. So in that, which could be found in Exodus 16:1-20, I learned to not worry about the morrow for it shall worry about itself and be thankful for the day I am in. God bless!

    You know it's hard to trust another human with your happiness,pain, heart, wants and/or needs when you're so use to giving it all to the Holy Spirit our Father God who art in heaven. For it is easy to give unto him because there is no judgment, deceit, betrayal of confidence or even feeling as though your emotions are being thrown back in your face for another's personal gain. You already know God is loyal, he is a wonderful counselor, the greatest friend who sticks closer than a brother, mother, sister, father, cousin, spouse and/or child! He is all those and so much more! I am grateful to know him and blessed to have this relationship with my heavenly father! Like I cannot say the same for those who are related to me for their relationship is far more different yet not on the same level. If that makes sense. My trust in them is not the same as my trust in God, not even close to making a homerun nor on first base. I'm just being honest. They may feel otherwise and may speak "their truth" but my God knows the battle I done had with them and still having honestly. I pray one day we all shall be on a mutual understanding and may God council and guide us to where he would like for us to be. However, it feels good to have that "deep trust" in God and know he is with you always. Yet there were times when I felt as though God was not present nor wanted to hear my voice but I prayed and worshiped him anyway. Now, I am no relationship expert nor am I hinting or seeking advice from those who specialize in this particular field; so please keep all advice and personal comments to yourselves. No disrespect, I am just speaking! My heart pours with sadness because even though I am in a relationship with my spouse; I do withhold some trust if not most from her. And it's not because I don't trust her which I do but only to a certain extent. I say this, for in the past and even so now at times, I don't trust the outcome of certain conversations we have regarding us because I feel she lingers on it for too long or it will be thrown back at me like a strike from a fast pitch machine and I'm not ready to swing. Like have you ever confided in a person or had a meaningful conversation and later on when they're mad at you or you don't give them what they ask for they throw your feelings back in your face for personal gain or place guilt upon you? Not saying my wife has done that but just giving an example. Even though in the past, we have, my wife and I, have gone through that in the beginning stages of our relationship. It was like a revolving door of the same scenario playing over and over. Lord knows I care truly and deeply for her; he knows my love for her is unreal to unconditional love that runs deep within my heart. But I struggle to trust her fully, she still loves me and takes really good care of me. I just love bringing what ails to the feet of my Father and letting him have the final say. I am very lucky, very fortunate to have her and still working to trust her more and more each day. I just don't like picking up things that I have left in God's hands. Lord, knows it has been hard because I have carried myself, carried my trio for so long with God's help; I do find it hard to let go of my pride a little. This my wife knows and respects. For she holds things from me and let Abba be Abba; for which I do understand and respect wholeheartedly. Many who have no good intentions or know us not well shall try to speak otherwise but no weapons formed against us shall prosper! I pray for my family day to day, moment by moment and know God hears while seeing all as he works in the midst of any trial and tribulation. Thank you Lord! Thank you for staying with me and guiding me through as each day goes by! Thank you for watching over us, being with us night and day; thick and thin showing us how wonderful, loving you are and how beautiful your spirit is! God thank you now and forever more in your son Jesus Christ name we pray, Amen!

A vessel that is broken is more open than a vessel made whole. A vessel made whole is more closed than a vessel that is broken. Which you can be? None can be both though why not use what is broken to create something new, something whole, something unimaginable! For one must believe in God, therefore broken is not lost, it is found and made new like Jesus who rose on the third day. A broken vessel is none like a broken bread of the last supper for which Jesus gave his body unto his disciples this day; for they drank and ate of what Jesus has been preparing them since they first met! For bread is the body given for all those who struggle to bow, or won't bow; wine is for the blood shed to forgive sins seen and unseen; done and not done! Jesus gave his life for all then, now and future generations! Believe or not; discourage or not; know truth or not but know he died for ALL! Not some, not most but for EVERYONE! Speak now or forever, hear thy saying know thine truth at heart within spirit that it is peace unto you no hurt harm or danger! Whether by ears and/or mind: no hurt, harm or danger. Come with ye own heart, lean unto the Lord understanding, appreciate his word from beginning to end; Jesus is first and last, Alpha and Omega! He is all that you cannot doubt nor fathom nor speak; for he is all! Speak now! Hear thy truth within spirit aside the loud there is quiet, aside the quiet there is peace, aside peace there is truth; aside of truth there is somber know the difference of becoming. Too bold? Yes. Too forward? No. Forwardness is truth though it can be twisted with intentions of one. One must know the difference of their worth, believe and accept who they are to know all forwardness is not truth let alone good for you. Given strength, given obedience, yet learning nothing but our own comfort and understanding; leaving the Lord's comfort and understanding on standby when we need or want him is a start of another sin looking to be forgiven! Despite personal feelings; regardless of mindless acts and/or thoughts to be of good courage; to be of great spirit not shamed of what is now heard. Keep the word of the Lord, close to thy Father, keep closer than thyself. For his grace is sufficient, his mercy is everlasting and his love is unconditional where conditional may lay on thine hearts which are not easily given nor is it easily hidden. What is faith? Why must we have faith? Faith equals: For Anyone Involved Trusting Him. We must first believe, then trust, then understand and then walk. When we believe, know we accept who God is and what he has and will do in our lives. When we trust, our hands are off the wheel and we have moved to the passenger side while Jesus takes control. When we understand, there is no doubt nor questions especially when God doesn't present either one. Know who or what is speaking. When we walk, we pick up our cross and follow; the valley may seem steep, dark and weary but Jesus is on the other side walking with us. Faith. Do remember, a vessel that is broken is more open than a vessel already made whole; though a vessel already made whole is more broken than a vessel broken which is open. God Bless.

The difference between us and Jesus, is that Jesus was more complete than we are and his purpose was more secure than our faith today. Even until the day of his crucifixion, Jesus's faith never wavered nor was he afraid! He did question and ask God to take the cup from him but Jesus, I believe, is more in love with God than most of us who claim to have love for God. As for us, being God's children through his son Jesus, still we struggle with our faith and to show true dedication to God. Even I myself question my love for God whether it is pure as the love Jesus has given. I feel as if I may not love God the same way he loves me. I say this because I do find myself asking God, well questioning God about things he has ordained, setting order in my life to which my faith is wavered. Of course, we all can admit even the "hardcore" Christians can admit they too have felt this way and questioned. You know it is an honor to be loved by someone who not only died for you but knew you before you were born and still said "yes" to the cross! Like, how amazing is that!? How wonderful and magnificent?! Many have and most have not taken this gift for granted! I know I did for most of my existence; especially in my twenties with barely any hunnies lol. Like I was lost in the sauce with no bread and hardly any water to quench my thirst. And yet, I bow with utmost respect, gratitude, love, obedience, and respect to him our Lord Jesus Christ. As my heart speaks fully with many thanks and my mind focused on his presence is truly a blessing outside of life itself! Those who look at me and life from the outside will never understand the joys within nor will they appreciate the testimony given. For those who do, I thank you! My life, my wilderness has not been the greatest but has been a battle which I am still amazed of the outcome. For he has been so good to me and my family which makes me wonder often why do he love me like this? Listen respect is important, because we are to respect one another and love each other as brothers and sisters. For Jesus has said John 13:34 "A new commandment I give unto you, That ye love one another; as I have loved you, that ye also love one another". But even brothers and sisters fight from time to time, if not all the time. This is natural human expected behavior. Naturally, I do not care of what they think nor have to say because they are not my Lord nor can they judge at the end of my time. I see it as this, we were all children once, we all grew up with different background stories but that is no excuse to be disrespectful nor hate one another! You see, kids don't get to choose their parents and parents don't get to choose their kids. A parent doesn't choose their child before birth but the child can choose to like and/or love their parents when they are born. Parents chose their kids because they carry, nurture, discipline, guide and all the responsibilities there are when you chose your child and they did not choose you. It is the simplest things such as a grasp on the finger, or a little smile upon gaze or even the comfort of being held by them really sets the tone of child view of their parents. It further sets a tone when the child talks back and shows no respect to their parents/guardians. Then, we are looking at many outcomes such as 25 to life. No child asked to be born yet they are here making their way to their own future. Though charity does start at home, I feel that somehow this saying gets misconstrued in a way or two. The old saying is simply self-explanatory and it is still misunderstood but holds much more value than four words. A child may be known to be "on their way" in life but can express or suppress what details of their journey. A child can ask to be guided then misguided, loved then unloved, treated right then mistreated mentally, physically, and emotionally. A child did not ask to be caught in between their parents "mishaps" or "drama" together or not. This can occur through any point and time of a child's life; written or unwritten who knows. But the saying of "charity starts at home", is the meaning of how the parent raises(trains up) the child and the outcome of the child's growth. Proverbs 22:6 "Train up a child in the way he should go: and when he is old, he will not depart from it". Let the child's future be more valuable, loving yet merciful and more wise than their parent's meaning of who they want them to be or become. Just as we were children once and grew to the best abilities our parents had to give; yet they were children once also and they grew to the best abilities their parents had to offer them. Amen, God bless.

    I don't understand people and I am sure it is not meant for me to understand. Like where is the trust in relationships when it comes to marriage? Where is respect when it comes to other people who are not kin to you? When does love become of an importance for those who have none? I am not understanding. Maybe it is not meant for me to understand. However, being no expert when it comes to relationships, I do know trust and communication of feelings are of importance along with loyalty. You know people can ask for a relationship but are they willing to commit fully and not partially? Are you willing to set aside some independence and let another take on what could be "overload" on you? Better yet, are you able to be "his feminine" or "hers"? Are you willing to be "her masculine" or "his" and not contradict one another? You know it's ok to set pride and independence aside, tear down your wall of "unwanted trusting of others". Relationships are not perfect, neither is love. Both are effortless and free flowing and wonderful to have. Many say "you have to put in work in order to make it last", really? What is my payment let alone monthly salary for this work I'm putting in to make this last? Then again, why ask for a vibe when you're not willing to match? I get, many people have different "vibes" and not all mesh well together but does blend beautifully. I mean, men mess up just as much as women mess up! Some take it farther than others and then cry for forgiveness or wonder why things don't go right in the next relationship. What I have learned in my past years of being with my wife is: Be careful with the words you say because they may not follow or match the actions you take. Meaning: don't say "I love you" then show you do not; don't say "I trust you" then keep your independence close like your enemies; don't say " we are in this together" but walk as if you're alone; and don't say " yes, I'll marry you" but out here being single. Be careful. For there will be a time when you do want to settle down but the life of your twenties and early thirties now hinder you from doing so. Know not everyone is out to get you let alone take advantage of you. It's ok to share but it's also ok to not share especially if the relationship you may have currently is not yet secure. I know some people are going to find this a "skeptical" saying but it is true. You can share in a relationship when you're fully committed, you can share with your spouse especially if you trust them and you married them; you can share. You can share with some friends you trust and there are some you can't because not everyone has your best interest at heart. You can share and be gracious while you do it; be joyful and have not a doubt in mind. It's ok to have some doubt but not to the point where it consumes you and you trust not a soul. If you believe you can't share with others then how can God share with you whether it's good, bad or indifferent? Think about it. Yes contradicting I know but that's why he gives us grace so we may do the same to those among us. Again, I am no expert but I do have my moments when I don't trust my spouse and I be wanting to but can't seem to find the grace to do so. In that, I just pray and let God be the one to hear and guide me on my doubting trust. Yet he has not failed to give me the courage to say what needs to be said. I honestly don't give all the details to my wife but just enough where she knows what bothers or what makes me happy or sad. And that my family is ok. For I gave it all to God to begin with, I didn't have to retell what was told but a glimpse just so she doesn't have to worry about me but pray over me. Some may not agree with this but honey, I honestly don't care. I say this respectfully: You can give God the worries of your life instead of giving it to another who may or not pray over you but can do a 360 and throw it back at you in some shape way or saying. I would rather let God handle it then let another human play with it. Like I said before: you can trust people and you can share your thoughts or ways of you but be careful especially if they don't have your best interest at heart. Be careful. God Bless.

In the 14 years of my service to you God (yes, I said fourteen) I am still trying to understand what is clearly not meant for me to understand. From what I have learned is that regardless of how another person may feel, do not let them change nor stir who God has you to become. Keep your peace and remain humble with a smile knowing no matter what they are going through you are not the cause. Do not let their darkness dim your light nor bring forth shadows that you may feel stirred, upset, angry in any way shape or form. Keep your light bright, so bright that their darkness has shadows which they do not like; shine bright as the sun on clear skies and the moon on starry night. Shine bright my child, smile and know I am with you always and forever Amen!

- Fourteen years of loyalty and undeniable love
- Fourteen years of forgiveness and truth unfold
- Fourteen years of mercy forever told and grace unmentioned
- Fourteen years of blessings, peace and resting souls
- Fourteen years of divine worship and everlasting praise
- Fourteen years of you my Lord God and son Jesus Christ
- Fourteen years of new beginnings and life fulfilled

There are many who may or may not be comfortable with some mentioned above while others are content with another person. I am eternally grateful, blessed and tremendously thankful to have you Lord God first and foremost in my life! My trio and wife may be the icing and fancy designs that make the cake look sooo delicious but you sir are the foundation which makes the cake stand tall, moist and delicate! Without you, this cake called life which I did not bake would be impossible to live! I would be dry and stale but Lord I thank you. Thank you and bless you forever and ever more. Fourteen years of you Lord God is more than enough and still is. I feel as though I can't thank you enough with or without a thousand tongues, my God I feel as though I can't thank you enough. But thank you, I adore, love and appreciate you! God Bless.

Have you ever just stood in front of a mirror and cried? Like literally watching yourself cry? I know it seems weird and no one likes to see themselves cry but have you? I have, on more than one occasion.

And when it was done, I thought to myself: "What am I crying about or who am I crying for? Am I crying for me or for those around me, not just my family? Am I crying out of gratitude, joy and peace?" One night, I was just crying, my heart was heavy and my mind was like all over the place. I felt as if I was crashing, spiraling out of control and I couldn't figure out why. So, I was telling my wife that I wasn't understanding what was going on around me and I felt like I was stuck. She says, "Well babe, you do have a lot going on around you and there are a lot of energies you're fighting but don't realize your fighting. And I get it because I feel the same way but I just pray about it". So have you ever felt like you were given good advice but also insulted at the same time? Lol, yep that was me! And I understood what she meant but still I was feeling "uneasy". She then told me to pray, take a moment, gather myself because dinner is almost ready and come downstairs. My wife hugged me and my arms fell to my sides as defeated. By this time I am in "stuck mode". Have you ever been in "stuck mode" like you can't move or speak? That was me in that particular moment. I just sat there and let my sourness consume whatever fight I thought was over. Dinner came around and of course no appetite but I didn't want the trio to worry because they don't like seeing me upset. I got up and there's a mirror attached to our dresser. I put some clothes away from laundry earlier that day and then I stopped. Looking straight into the mirror I began to cry more deeply and the pain was greater than before. My heart was screaming, my ears were pounding sounds of whoosh and my mind was on a series of: "I don't know who I am. I don't see what others see in me that I should have seen in myself. God who am I?! What am I?! Who or what I should be or become?! Talk to me! I am lost, am I not worthy to be found?" Like so much just coming out one after another and then my head starts to hurt, you know migraine. I was done. I didn't want to eat nor could I force myself. The grip I thought I gripped has slipped completely. And honestly guys, I have battled with myself for the past 20 years! Not knowing my purpose in life, who I am supposed to be in this world outside of a mother of three children and wife to a woman which society frowns upon our relationship. They judge then they don't judge. It's very comical backwards and yet still a trending matter. However, for 20 years I have struggled with myself. I have struggled with marks upon my body which my wife loves but I am unsure because they are old and new scars faded visibly. I have struggled with what the world has deemed "depression and anxiety" but to me I am just going day by day, moment by moment; kids are going to be kids, raise them the best way you can with the Lord's advice and not others. I am newly struggling with my ears whooshing which society has also deemed to be part of the "stress and anxiety" crew called tinnitus. I promise if it is not one thing it's another lol. Yet I feel as if I am hearing the thumping of a bass drum or loud claps of palm hands; or even the loud stomps of marching but muffled. I do not know and yes this may be weird "theories" to you but to me it feels real. I know not what to make of it at times and yet I am still here. In that, I often wonder why? God your hand, your healing hand holds me, your unconditional love surrounds me and your everlasting grace and mercy is upon me! I thank you, God! I thank you for the acceptance I now come to terms with and still struggle in a way. I thank you for your guidance through all my transitions of embracing myself and loving me for me. Trying to. I thank you Lord, for truly being a great wonder and finding me worthy enough to be your child. Though I feel as though I am not worthy because of my life I am living yet I love you deeply and willing to be eunuch for such a cause. But am I here to appease the world of their views of your word or to be whom ye has called me to become that is your word? I know not, nevertheless I thank you Father! As we lift our hands to heaven and let our voices sing, Amen!

You know it is a rare love for someone to actually love you regardless of what the world sees you or how the world sees you; this person loves you for you! They don't ask you to change nor do they imply by looking for another with those changes! They just look at you as if you're the only one in this world and are amazed by the grace God has placed upon you because God loves you for you. Which makes this person's love for you even more special and more worthy to praise God! Give him all praise, all the glory, show forth all joy and all happiness for he created you! He created me! Do you know how much of a blessing this is?! This is a better blessing than any amount of money you can receive, any amount of land you can acquire; this is far greater than saying "I do!". Like this is unbelievably amazing! A rare love is hard to come by especially in the time we live in today and even back then. A rare love is hard to come by, it is hard to appreciate, it is hard to accept because it's a "foreign feeling". I say this because this "foreign feeling", we are not used to, we don't know how to cherish once in our presence. It's just like the love, grace and mercy God has bestowed upon us for many, many, many years! This doesn't feel good to us, makes us uncomfortable and we don't even want it let alone embrace it! So, this means we don't want God's love, grace and mercy because we are not comfortable with it. And who says we have to be comfortable? Why not just be of comfort to his presence instead of shunning him at the first sight, touch or hear? Not comfortable you say, not "feeling good" you speak, not understanding you heard. Well, sorry to break it to you but you get what you get and he provides according to his purpose, his comfort, his grace, and his mercy which all equals his TIMING! It is good for us to wait and receive when it is given. God is a great wonder and does work in mysterious ways. But what makes people think he has to work in "their wonder" and/or "their mysterious ways"? Think about it, shame the devil for he will try to say otherwise. Know truth. Know God's truth and really listen to his word as you read. For he will speak to you and give you the discernment you need and not the discernment you "feel" you should have. True discernment lies within the voice of God not the voice of man. It comes from God's faith and trust he has within you not the faith and trust you have in others or what they may say about you! And you know, I believe God is trying his best to sustain all that is good, destroy all that is bad and restore all that is indifferent for the greater good. I do believe we were all placed upon this earth to be who he wants us to be, not what the people say we should be. And yet it is up to us, his children to know the difference!

We must know to take accountability for our actions. We must know the word according to God's understanding, not our own twelve thousand versions. Like come on now. We were made in the likeness of his image and given the likeness of his knowledge but as servants not God. For his thoughts are higher than ours and his ways are greater than ours. God didn't allow "free will" to stay just so we as his children could mess it up even more! And yet we are now out of control and will be corrected according to Jesus coming back. Be ready, be of good faith and courage. Know a rare love is hard to come by. God's love is hard to come by. You just have to be open to accept, embrace and love in return. God Bless!

So, I may or may not touch a few nerves with what I'm about to say next. But have you ever felt or even thought about what God truly wants from his people? Like what life he wants us to live whether it's purely and not just "winging it"? Thinking or living how we want but asking forgiveness along the way. Pastors and ministers for example:

some live by the word and others live by freedom. Those who live by the word live for the Lord yet experience temptation which is hard for them to break in their eyes but overcome the obstacles with God's grace. Those who live freely do as the world presents and allow temptation to overcome them but constantly ask for God's forgiveness just so they can go back through temptation and ask again. And yet I feel there is some judgment in that and neither of us have the right to pass let alone condemn those who choose either/or maybe even both. I believe God does want us to be curious about him but live our lives freely. I also believe he wants to see the choices we make will either teach us or break us. Most importantly, teach us! If we are broken then we must have learned something from that brokenness therefore he has taught us the lesson we needed to learn. He has given us a contrite heart: A heart that has been broken and we no longer want to do what we used to do but surrender ourselves to God. The ones who live by the word are often broken yet made whole because of the lesson they were taught which God has revealed within their spirit. The ones who live free are to be taught a lesson with every mistake they made and will continue to be at God's mercy but for how long shall he cover us with forgiveness before he turns his face from us? Those who live by the word yet also live freely, have truly seen the goodness of God and know the true nature of " he will never leave me nor forsake me"; for if I keep my focus on him I shall not have to live in the bondage which the world has created. I walk by faith and not by sight for I seek him daily and consult with him always. God does not want us to start and then stop seeking him, this I know and have learned many times before and even now. Seek God always! Even when it's cold, dark and you're feeling alone, still seek him! When it's bright sunny, birds chirping and you're dancing all around, still seek God! He welcomes you and he welcomes all that you are and all that you have! His wonder is a bit difficult to understand but it is not meant for us to understand just to embrace the grace and love within it. Give him all the glory and praise! Seek God and only God with all your heart, keep your mind open and your ears listening. Trust, it is worth the travel, he is worth the experience of being fulfilled! He is worthy to be at all times! I know it is easier said than done, this I know but trust me the faith you have in God; the love you show for Christ is not only worth living but it is worth being free to live. God, we thank you for this life you have given us to not only live in your word but to be free. Do not feel bound to the ways this world has created within itself where it now utilizes your word to conform and set the ways of its own twisted laws. To be free to love, learn, and live without a shadow of a doubt and to continue to walk by faith without the sight of the world is a blessing. My God, I thank you for your true teachings and guidance. I know there are many versions of the word Lord, but I believe what ye has written before can be understood by the heart which lies within you but has the wisdom and discernment of you, heavenly Father. And that comes by prayer, fasting and faith. We all struggle from time to time but we know what we must do to be equipped with the true knowledge given at the time of Adam and Eve. My Lord, I ask thee for you, your guidance, your wisdom, your understanding and furthermore your truth of the life we are to be living. I ask thee O' God please reveal thy truth so the world may be restored to where you would have first intended. I believe this is not it and I furthermore believe you my God are not done with us yet. I pray for peace in everyone's heart and mind on the day Jesus comes; so they will not be frantic nor stuck and truth shall flow of their actions and words spoken against thee. In Jesus name I pray, Amen. God bless.

To have a spiritual talk with your children is most delightful. However, a child's mind is a curious read yet a wondrous understanding. Children have their own spiritual journey, their own encounters with God. The way they explain it may seem like a "fairy tale" but really that's what it is to them. My trio have their own explanations when we talk about God and daily life. My youngest, who is seven, her experience with Jesus as she says is most real but it is hard for her to explain but she believes! The crazy part about this, when she explains her encounters with Jesus, she describes him so vividly and not text book or television versions. Her view of him has been the same since before we even introduced any bibles or tv shows about Jesus. Crazy? I know but it's so real. Anywho, this makes it hard but easy for me to understand and believe what she tells me and my wife about her dreams she had. And that is the most beautiful part because children try their best to explain on an "adult level" but really speaking from a child's mind. I find that to be amazing yet "don't hurt yourself" lol experience. I have to tell her to explain it the best way she can even if it's her way. Now my oldest, who is twelve, can see figures which to her are scary but to me it's like "congratulations you are gifted/anointed" so walk in it. Lol. No, she is in disbelief because she doesn't know who these figures are and where they come from. As I explain, I try my best to with God's guidance, I explain that whoever it is she sees and how she must pray to God for his true clarity, his wisdom on the matter. I tell her only God can interpret what it is you see and give you the understanding of what it means. And as I try to explain, she is like terrified but curious as to why she has this gift; and all I can say to her is go to God and pray for his wise counsel and I will pray over you so no other can intercede and try to take or destroy the plan God has for you. Now my son, who is nine, feels a certain presence whether it's good or bad but has a hard time deciphering between the two. He loves music and can move to the beat while creating his own. But he does know when good is around because he doesn't like the feeling(uncomfortable) and he knows when bad is around because he likes the feeling(comfortable). I have to teach him the difference between good and bad feelings which he is still learning. I encourage him to pray when he feels uncomfortable so he knows that feeling is the presence of God and he is newly learning what God's presence feels like. I teach him to rebuke what is comfortable because he then gets angry for no reason and/or harms those who have done nothing to him because that is not "ok" to do. I teach him to know when God is here and when the Devil is tempting because he is young and is learning the word of God day by day. And that's the thing, children can be easily tempted at a young age but also anointed at a different age. A child tempted at a young age can be corrupted or lead down a path which causes them their future. A child anointed at a young age can be most tempted than a child already tempted but has grace to overcome. It is up to the village to raise the child to be who God has called them to be! Again, Proverbs 22:6 " Train up a child in the way he should go: and when he is old, he will not depart from it." It is up to the child's parent or guardian to ensure the child knows the voice of God and knows his presence is of comfort and not comfortability! That's what I am still learning and my trio are learning. Your are never too old to stop learning, especially when it comes to God. I have moments where I have to question and pray for answers. Not judging anyone. Just speaking from my own experience of my own testimonial journey. This life have not been easy but joyous! I may not be able to recall every bit and piece of my life but I do recall when it is called to be spoken about. This is what I have traveled with my faith and my children. How you travel is your business and your testimony you can share at your convenience. Man, I love spiritual talks with my family! We may not be your "average family" but we are a family put together by God. For this I am grateful! It is so much love and joy to sit, talk, play cards or board games; just talk about each other's day or what God has shown us through other people; how gracious and merciful he has been and continues to be. What a wonderful experience to have and enjoy. I am blessed to live long enough to see it! Thank you Lord! I am sure you will feel differently and criticize saying " this is not of God nor is it in his word" but honestly, have you even taken the time to ask let alone wait for his understanding of his word? I have. I do, every single day. And you know, in that I ask him to remove all that is not for me and not of him! Nevertheless, he still takes care of us. He still shows up at the perfect time when called. He has removed those I did not expect to be moved nor to ever speak to again. The same with my wife and that tore her up! But nevertheless, he comforted her and is guiding us to where he desires for us to be. So do not judge what you do not know. It is an honor to be spoken by God not only at a young age but at any age, any point of your life whether it seems good or bad to you but God sees it differently. Amazing he is and miraculous he has been. Forty days of wilderness, forty nights of prayer is soon to come. God Bless.

Can faith make you happy or can it make you sad? Both? How about, can faith cause you to live or to die? Both? Honestly, faith is "worth living" but can also create an "identity of death". Many people will choose one or the other depending on the circumstances of their lives. Some will disagree with this saying while others contemplate on whether this speaks some form of truth. Faith is "worth living" by what is unexpected rather than what is expected. For God, in my opinion, is an unexpected God. He shows in a timing that is not ours but yet he is right on time. For whatever situation you have prayed about God has not seen it to be answered immediately but in due time. So just know he is a God of unexpectancy. Faith is also "identity of death" because some people, if not many, will live by what is expected from society, meaning the world and make it their identity all the while fighting the truth of who they really are. You're expected to be this person just so you don't feel the judgment from others who see you physically rather than spiritually. Relationships for instance, you are expected to be this same person, when first met, from start until God do you part. The problem is people do change through the course of their relationship which could result in good change or bad change depending on how their partner sees it. People change in height, weight, style, even character and personalities change. So, why expect this person to be the same? If you cannot accept change, then why even expect anything from another person: love, friendship, business partnership and/or sales? If you cannot accept change from your own son, daughter, friend or even yourself then why ask God to change you or them? Make me a clean heart? Why ask him to help you overcome the change that is natural and unexpected? Faith is "worth living" because you are worth the love, the respect, the gratitude, the grace, the mercy, the courage, even the fight you cannot see but God sees and have already won for victory is mine! Amen, my God! Faith is also "identity of death" because there are some who choose comfortability over comfort, they choose strife and not deal with it, just build up more and more. They choose to be tested yet fail but pass in the eyes of their flesh. They choose to be the same regardless if it hurts others or even themselves. They choose to be what the world expects them to be and/or do because their identity is made comfortable to them. Love God with thy lips but curse thee with thine heart and mind. How so? You don't want nor feel the change God has placed because his comfort is not enough. Now this is my opinion: Judas betrayed Jesus because his position as a disciple was not enough and in some circumstances he did not agree with Jesus' teachings. Confused, yes he was but the power he was charged with by Jesus didn't sustain enough value, not serving him any purpose but for Jesus this was magnifying the work of God. So many interpretations but what is truth and what is false? My God I beg of thee to chastise me if my words are false or even deceiving in thine eyes. For ye may take me and leave me blind that I may speak of any lies. I am asking you Lord, for no man, no woman, no preacher, no prophet, no disciple, no christian can judge me except my Lord Jesus Christ himself! I pray thee, my God, Amen! We all have our own understanding/interpretation when it comes to the bible. I guess that's why there are so many versions of it(shoulder shrugs). I do pray in time, God will reveal his truth and show us his word himself. For man has gone a bit…overboard with no life jacket to float. However, God bless.

In addition to what was written, regarding my own faith was most revealing. For I have opened myself unto the Lord and spoke what was deep in troubling. I said, "Lord, please forgive me if I am unable to recall your word by flow as most of those who follow you yet I carry my cross upon my shoulders daily and led by your words I follow thee. I follow thee deep in the valley where death has tried to succumb me, deep in the valley where Satan has often tempted me and in that I have succumbed to many but delivered by few. I may not be the Christian most say or preach you have to be in order to be accepted in your kingdom but I know my heart belongs to thee. My cross, I carry with you my Lord by my side, I walk with thee". And you know what he revealed to me while I prayed? God said to me, "There are many who "quote" my word yet leave their cross, there are many who preach my word yet greed for gold and silver, there are many who love my word yet disobey the commandments and repent not. For Satan has quoted my word many but has fallen from my kingdom thousands, he has tempted plenty yet kept their souls as trophies and depleted their spirits for victories; Satan may have been one of the fallen but have obeyed according to what was written. He may have deceived for his own personal gain but soon he will lose all that he reigns and more. For this world will become no more". Can you walk the very same faith you speak? Can you literally walk in faith and not lose the faith you talk when life throws you curveballs? I understand we all have a past yet we choose to ignore and portray as though it never existed. Yet it exists and can find its way to your present by those who do not want you to live your future. Amen, my God. Many people will have this trouble once the trumpets begin. Many people will be on their knees begging saying "Jesus please!" before he even speaks. Many people and even I have talked much but walked very little! I mean, can you handle faith? Can we be honest? Let's be honest! People will say they have all this faith yet walk as if they are broken in many ways. Which you could be but why show that you are? I may not look like what I have been through but my God I have overcome. It is easier to agree than to actually be truthful and honest with yourself. Faith comes with actions not speaking, faith is all walk no need to talk let alone see to where he is taking you. For we walk by faith and not by sight, right? Yet many of us would rather see where we are going: whether it's to have or to hold or to spend and to be bold. Either way, why must we know when the author of our lives needs us not to know but to trust who or what we do not see. It's ok to say you have faith, letting it be known is fine but overstating with no walking is fear. I say this because, fear will have you feeling as though you won't overcome the faith you speak so "heavy" about when temptation decides to smack you dead in your mouth. So, can you handle talking faith as well as walking in faith? Do you know the difference? The difference is talking faith is just speaking with no action in hopes everything will come to you; walking in faith is putting in the work so God can see how committed you are. James 2:26 "For as the body without the spirit is dead, so faith without work is dead also". So, if God was to take his spirit back then what are we? Dead. If we are to speak faith and not walk in it, then that will make us dead also. Right? Come on saints! Don't get quiet on me now. You know God's timing is perfect just how the unexpected is made perfect also. Not everything in life will be expected including "faith talk" will be known as blessing. You know what is a blessing? The unexpected. The unexpected is the greatest joy, love, peace and happiness you will ever receive as a true blessing! Jesus himself was made perfect yet a man. Man was made good but corrupted themselves by temptation to be known as imperfect. Though man is made good, Jesus was made perfect therefore God's will and purpose are unexpectedly perfect. Listen, I know I have my kinks and giggles but some will say "hookups". But my heart and mind do battle with each other daily. For my heart is with Christ yet my mind is like "Listen, let's just see for yourself and go from there."; my heart is like "Noooo!" and my spirit is like "Bro, you bout to get jumped!". And it's a nonstop argument but there is some common ground if that makes sense. We all have this I'm sure, if not, then now you know. No one is made perfect, no human is made perfect, only good! We were made good in the eyes of the Lord but deemed bad by the temptation of Satan who is known bad. There are some who struggle to be Christ-like, not everyone will be like Christ. Why? Because people find it impossible and honestly no one wants to endure what Christ has done. For the temptation of the world is easy to touch, easy to hear, easy to understand yet be confused because it is what Satan expects. Hmmhmm my God! Let any man who has an ear let him hear! This speaks so many volumes, who is willing to turn up and listen? Who is willing to open up and say, "Yes Lord, I have an ear let me hear!"? My God, my Lord Jesus! How can we give Satan the expectation but refuse to accept the unexpected from God? You see, you can have everything of this world but the moment you close your eyes; what is of this world stays and your soul belongs to the Devil and your spirit goes back to God. Meaning the breath you breathe goes back to God yet the flesh returns to dust. Have you forgotten who created you? And yet we act as though the world is all we got! Man, BYE! In all honesty, the world can have itself and I rather have God than let the world have me. God Bless.

Faith is a true substance of God's work revealed and the truth we do not see. We may speak of having truth and wanting to know the truth but can we receive truth without first contradicting ourselves? It is like the things we do see, we want to control but fail to realize there is more to battle that is unseen. The things we do see are not of faith, but of what we want to be yet true faith lies within God and his word. It is of our own interpretation of faith itself that we do not understand the word God has spoken. I believe, the things we do see are of fantasy what we expect the kingdom of God to be yet we do fail to realize the kingdom of God is seen through the true belief of Jesus Christ, our Lord and Saviour. What does lie before us is in fact a delusion, a cover to what really lies beneath the surface. What lies beneath is the true revelation of ourselves and honestly to most will be too scary to reveal. Our eyes will be unable to bare what is seen. Truth be told, the true desires of what God has originally seen will be considered unlawful of this world. And you know this mystery is highly mysterious yet an amazing wonder that can only be revealed by God himself. I love it! I love the fact the human body was not created to be explored or compared to other living creatures that have been created. I love that we come from dirt and not from animals as "science" tries to complete theories. I love us! I love me! And I have accepted what God has created me to be. Why can't you? What is so hard to believe that you were made to be an image of God's mind? God has designed us as an image of his liking not ours to be picked, pride and misconstrued or made up. What we have done amongst each other is sad and horrible! We have truly divided ourselves from the image of God and he is not pleased. Faith is more than words and is more than actions! Faith is God who is bigger than a definition in the dictionary or bible! I believe God has created us to live in peace but with the right decisions of "free will". Satan pushed limits and we created our own disasters. God created us to live in his image by his laws and yet man has taken what was written and made it more about his own image and laws. I mean, we couldn't agree on the image of Christ for crying out loud! Man hath become more comfortable, has lost their sight more than a man who was born with no sight. And yet the one born with no sight has more of God's image than the one born with sight. One born with ears hears very little than one born with no ears hears a lot. Just as one whose voice speaks silent spoken much then one whose voice speaks loud has spoken none. Amen! I get no one will understand nor do I expect. I do expect Abba to be Abba! I don't want to change him or his commandments, I am not Jesus. I do pray we all come to a bow when time comes yet before hand let us come to an agreement, understanding of what was asked before Calvary. To love one another as ye love yourself; as you love Christ. I feel the assignment of the world is the same but has different meanings. No one wants to be wrong, everyone has to right in his own eyes. You know, I don't expect to be right because 90% of the time I am declaring myself wrong. And yet God has said he will give us the words to speak according to him. Even though we may feel like a child, he will still give us the words that need to be spoken. Jeremiah 1:6-7 " Then said I, Ah, Lord God! behold, I cannot speak: for I am a child. But the Lord said unto me, Say not, I am a child:for thou shalt go to all that I shall send thee, and whatsoever I command thee thou shalt speak." Even Jesus said in Matthew 10:16-20 "Behold, I send you forth as sheep in the midst of wolves: be ye therefore wise as serpents, and harmless as doves. But beware of men: for they will deliver you up to the councils, and they will scourge you in their synagogues; And ye shall be brought before governors and kings for my sake, for a testimony against them and the Gentiles. But when they deliver you up, take no thought how or what ye shall speak: for it shall be given you in that same hour what ye shall speak. For it is not ye that speak, but the Spirit of your Father which speaketh in you." God, the author and creator of us all, dictates our speech and orders our steps. Believe. God bless.

As Faith Walk comes to a close, the journey we have taken seems to have raised questions along the way. Though these questions are more like comments, I am led to speak on the matter at hand. I am aware that many of you do not agree with what was spoken let alone feel as though I am on a path that is not of God. However, the path I am on is my own and this I believe God has created for me. As I have mentioned before, growing up I was taught that God has only created man, woman and beast, thus this is true but he did not ordain for anything else outside of those three. For he only meant for male and female to be together not male and male or female and female. I have seen many speculators testimony about this and yet have wondered why the anger emotion behind what they were speaking. I felt as though they were speaking in anger or being firm because this will displease God and if we should continue in that manner, we shall surely not enter the kingdom of heaven. Passion, I get it. As I grew older, my curiosity became more detective. Of course I did go in the way I was taught but often felt as though I did not belong and yet I went along with it. The times I tried with men I felt used and unwanted. The times I didn't try and it came naturally I still felt used, unwanted and ultimately not enough. To be honest, I never wore any makeup such as foundation, concealers and all that junk. I only put on eyeliner, those eye glitter shadows and like lip gloss lipstick. And that was rare because I hardly went anywhere nor seen the point to do so. When I did, I did it because of those I hung out with said to do so. There were many nights when I went out with friends and went home alone. I had a few spur nights where I did have company but that was a "one night stand". My first child, my daughter, I had when I was 21 and she was conceived from a night where I should've just stayed home but friends were having a get together and insisted I come out for a few. Mind you this was days perhaps a week or so after I tried to kill myself, so I really wasn't in a good headspace. However, the night it happened it was snowing really bad and I was drunk walking in the snow with the guy because his cousin insisted he do. However, I found out I was pregnant and nine months later child #1. My 2nd child was conceived from a "one night stand" and that truth be told should not have happened and yet I have my son. That night was insane because the guy I thought wanted me ended up spinning me so I left with my friend and her dude and his friend. Of course I was the driver, I dropped my friend and her dude off and his friend asked to drop him off which was along the way to me going home anyway. Get to his house, he's trying to talk to me and I'm waiting for him to get out my car so I can go! lol Like I'm already irritated but being nice just talking and listening and before you know he's on me kissing, getting in my pants then five minutes later he's out the car and I'm driving home. Didn't know what to think of that situation because I was drunk/high and stuck on the incident prior to that one. After some time has passed, like a month or so, I find myself pregnant but in denial. Mind you, I carried on with my life, drinking and smoking as if I wasn't with child. I know terrible this I can admit so save your comments for someone else please. Eight months later my son was born, tiny but healthy and I didn't know it was a boy until the day I went into labor. I hadn't seen any doctors or anything. But you know God is good! He kept him healthy and alive for a reason. I went through postpartum depression and had to undergo some counseling because honestly I didn't want another child. And yet here he was so chocolatey, healthy and handsome. I soon got it together, lost my house and job in the process but I was able to pull it together. My grandmother was my biggest supporter at the time. She was always there to give advice, prayer, she even watched the kids while I went on interviews for work. She really has been a blessing to me and my children. I thank God for her daily. Now, I'm back on my feet: job, new house, new mindset, still going the way of male and female. It was the summer/fall season when I tried online dating. The apps I tried were like Tinder, Tango or BlackPeople.com you know places like that. I matched with a few but only spoke to one maybe two out of both apps. And that, honestly, was sketchy because at that time I really didn't have a vehicle and I wasn't about to have anybody knowing where I lived, especially if we not on that type of time. However, things were going pretty good. I met a guy on Tango or Tinder, can't remember which one but it was coo. We talked for quite a bit and I had got a car which made it easier to find work. Then I found out the guy was messing with another female so I got upset and started talking to another guy on Tinder and we hooked up for a night. And that I regretted it because I did it out of anger and wasn't thinking. However, life happened once again. I lost my job and it sucked because it was around holiday time and the weather back then was real winter weather. On top of that, I found out I was pregnant again and of course I was happy but bitter because of how the pregnancy came about. So me and the kids went to stay with my sister until I was able to get another job but I still had my house but no heat at the time. So we went over there, work was hard to come by like nobody was hiring and mind you I have a degree in Business Management but not hirable because of the lack of experience. (eye roll) Anywho, of course tax season rolls around and the weather starts to break. I paid my rent and bills. I went back home to find my house had flooded. A pipe had burst from the below zero weather and I didn't know where the main valve to the water line was. The house didn't have a basement. I called the landlord at the time, he said it was in the back of the house. I told him it wasn't, he got even more mad and hung up. The maintenance guy comes out and opens up the bottom of my closet floor and walks downstairs to the crawl space where the water main valve was. I said how did you know it was down there and not me? He said he has been working on this house for years and the previous, previous owner told him where it was. I said that would have been nice to know when I first moved in! However, the landlord was not cooperating when it came to fix the damages done to the floors which I agreed to pay but he was not communicating with me. A month passed and I had a new landlord that knew nothing about what happened to the property. I was told I would get a call back but nobody called me back. I went to the office and was told I had a previous rent balance, I told them I paid my rent and showed proof of payment. I was told again I would be contacted but no one again contacted me. A few weeks later I was out of a home, the locks were changed as well as the landlord changed again. I felt myself breaking on top of being pregnant. My sister offered we stay with her until I can find another place. Finding a place was like finding a job. My 3rd child was born months later. I had found work but was let go because I was pregnant so soon to give birth. Holidays were coming around again. I found work but had no vehicle, it had broke down so I had to junk it. Holidays came and gone, there I was working but no place of my own. I felt my sister was tired of us even though she didn't say it but her actions spoke it. There was a night, I was in my sister's basement, I just laid on the couch and cried. Looking out the window I just cried a deep failing cry. In that moment I prayed and asked God, is this life for me? Why would you bring me this far to become this? Why would you not just let me go all them years ago when I did try to kill myself? Why? Still crying, I fell asleep, woke up, fed the baby girl and went right back to sleep. The next few weeks I was silent, really didn't have much to say but folks had lots to say about me. However, the new year came and a friend had told me about subsidized housing and where I can apply because they will go by my income. I applied and did the intake interview. A couple months later, I got the call for a place which had become available. I went to look at it, spoke to the landlord and was able to get my keys that day. I moved a couple weeks later because they replaced the carpet and repainted the home. The trio was happy and that made me feel good. I thanked God and asked for his forgiveness. Because I questioned him while he was in the process of my solution. I didn't even know as we don't but it was the frustration of the situation and not coming to him sooner. Trying to do everything on my own and all I had to do was let go and let God! Listen, five years later and yes still going with the flow of male and female but not caring and just getting what I want and that's it. On top of losing my grandmother a year after being on my own and having changed jobs twice but no more pregnancies. I gave up on the dating life. Especially after the last guy I dealt with, that was the icing on the cake for me.

Like, I don't need to control anybody, I can barely control myself and yet he had the nerve to say I was trying to control him. Boy! Anywho, I gave up on the dating scene, especially online and "friends" trying to set me up dating. I was done. I said Lord, I love you and I thank you, but furthermore I am content with it just being you, me and the trio. This is not working for me and idk what could I be doing or saying wrong for no male to find me to be a good thing, a wife. Is that not what your word is teaching us? Did I miss something? And God said "Yes, you're missing me, remember what ye asked me long ago?" That took me out. To where I had a dream that I wrote a letter to God, placed it in my bible and left it there. Mind you this bible was at my grandmother's house which I no longer had access to but I soon remember what I wrote: "Dear God, I would like to have my own: My own house, my own car, my own career, my own family and my own companion. These things is what I would like according to how you see. Thank you, I love you!" My heart cried while my mind pondered. Trying to achieve without first seeking wise counsel, seeking God. One night I prayed and asked God to not only forgive me but to give me direction. If I must stand still, then keep me still, If I must go then where do you want me to go? I didn't realize in that moment he had already ordered my steps. I was walking a new path. So my wife and I were coworkers/associates before we even became friends. The feelings I had for her I shunned and prayed telling God this is not of him, take these feelings away for your word says this is an abomination in your eyes. Like there's no way you would approve of this God, I am going to fall hard in the pit. And that was my problem, telling God, the author, about what was written. I felt the cold shoulder from God. When I mean cold shoulder I mean so cold like the North pole with a -100 degree cold. I got demoted from my job, I was supervisor and ended up going to school for healthcare. All the while still praying, still being my wife's friend not trying to engage in anything serious. I did a little fornicating but that was rare temptation. I knew I couldn't do it again. I even had a driver ask for my number but I didn't want to nor did I want him. I just felt like I shouldn't be engaging, especially having these unwanted feelings. I remember one night, I was at work, kids at daycare, I sat in my truck and just talking to God but mostly apologizing because I was not trying to offend him in any shape, way or form. I was just speaking on what I have been taught for so many years and still it's being taught until this day. I said Lord, you made male and female, that is how it's supposed to be right? If not, then what the heck went wrong with Genesis? I have always heard that your word shall not return unto you void, your word is your word. I do not want to go against you or Christ. So please help me, help the world understand. What is it you want? What truth has not been spoken? Please God, I need you! And I realize now, being another five years later, fully married, trio healthy and work/vehicle has been steady: that help was the key lost in translation. Yall, I've been on crazy yet curious faith and for the Lord to finally answer a question from five years ago until today...I am truly blessed! You see, when God created Eve, he created her to help Adam, it was Adam who took it upon himself to call Eve woman and his wife. Never in that moment when

Adam said this God corrected him nor did he speak otherwise; God was silent. Just because he was silent doesn't mean he agreed. It was then after the deception is when God confirmed Eve to be his wife because Adam listened to her and did not first consult with God. But Adam blamed Eve for a choice he made even though he could have seeked wise counsel. Just because you're handed something doesn't mean you have to accept it. I can hand you a bottle of water but that doesn't mean you have to drink it. Same you can hand me a slice of pizza, doesn't mean I have to eat it. They both had a choice and yet they chose to disobey. Sounds familiar? We choose to be disobedient yet cry for deliverance. Meaning, we choose to act first and seek wise counsel later. How does that work? It doesn't. But you know for what God puts together, no man can tear apart. I believe the Devil tried to tear Adam and Eve apart. He didn't like the fact that not only he gets banished from heaven but God had the nerve to create another species outside of him and his brothers. You know God, he is very creative and funny. In Job 1:6 when the sons of God gathered before him, including

Satan; there was no mention of daughters only sons. Now, unless I am not spiritual enough, why is it long after Genesis, there are no daughters of God only sons? I have heard that the Devil would not have tried to tempt Adam for he was like his brothers in heaven but Eve was a different breed unlike the rest of them. Not only physically but mentally also. She was the first of all women both in earth and heaven. This we can dive deep into later. There are times I have read in the bible, and some of you also, where God not only wanted to take some people out but actually took some people out! You see, God is not only all knowing, loving and powerful; he is also forgiving and gracious enough to let us continue life. These days, family, count your blessings and stop judging in places you have no authority. You don't know a person until their story has been told and in that you still have no authority to judge them but love them as Jesus loves you! God bless.

Faith Walk is a blessing with many challenges which I, myself have endured, learned and am grateful. For I would not be the person I am at this moment. The amount of growth within me has shown outward and many can not seem to understand let alone placing their own answers to the question why. I thank my Lord Jesus for his sacrifice many many years ago but most importantly I thank God, for he has given the greatest gift no man or woman dare to ask. For he hast given us his son, Jesus, to forgive our sins before we were born let alone to repent the sins we have yet committed. God created me in an image of him yet knowing the trials of life before I encountered them. I praise thee for all to which have been sacrificed not only by the blood of my Saviour but the mercy given to many who feel they have done no wrong. Thank you my father, for you are with me and have shown me so much yet I be feeling so unworthy of you. Abba, Father, please forgive me for when my faith has wavered and I questioned thy purpose for me. I am of flesh though still learning to be more of spirit in your liking with your guidance. I pray those who have read and received all that is said here; take into heart and reflect on their own lives and judge not anybody around them. Faith Walk, you are a blessing I shall carry with me always. For our journey together does not end here, she carries on to a place of wilderness and nights covered by our Lord Jesus Christ whose blood continues to shed. Whose mercy continues to cover us daily yet we take thee for granted. The choices we make is the outcome we must face. Though we must seek ye first the kingdom of heaven and not rely on our own understanding. We must seek Christ, pick up thy cross and follow him! Our lives are different, we were not created to live the same, this I believe. For if we were, our steps would be ordered the same and our physical appearance would be of the same as the blood in our veins. We were created to help one another, love one another, multiply and be fruitful together and not be apart. For we are to be of one body with many members including Christ of the Holy Spirit. 1 Corinthians 12:12-14 "For as the body is one, and hath many members, and all the members of that one body, being many, are one body: so also is Christ. For by one Spirit are we all baptized into one body, whether we be Jews or Gentiles, whether we be bond or free; and have been all made to drink into one Spirit. For the body is not one member, but many." Let a man that has an ear, let him hear. We are all created by God who is one Spirit, for his breath breathes in our lungs day and night. We bleed the same yet look different but we treat each other as we look and that is not what Christ nor God has been trying to teach us in the bible. And yet, we do as we please and feel as we may. Family, pray. He's coming. I thank thee all for listening, may the heavens continue to smile upon you always. In Jesus name I pray: Let thy will be done, let thy purpose be fulfilled and thank you for thy mercy has been granted, Amen. God bless.

It Is Finished